TRUMP

HOW HE CAPTURED THE TRUMP WHITE HOUSE

TRUMP

HOW HE CAPTURED THE TRUMP WHITE HOUSE

by

Mitch Wolfe

Published by **Marnie Kay**

For any information regarding permission contact
Mitch Wolfe via **www.mitchwolfe.com**

Printed in the United States of America

Paperback ISBN – 978-1988364-02-5

eBook ISBN – 978-1-988364-03-2

Book cover design by
www.designisreborn.com

reborn
Design Redefined

WITH GREAT APOLOGIES TO WB YEATS

THE SECOND COMING OF TRUMP

The people no longer hear CNN.
The left, right and centre cannot hold.
The black sun king is ignored
While his screeching heir
Abhorred.

Somewhere from the streets of Queens
With head so weird and hands so yuge

A very rough beast
Its reality hour nigh

Strides to the White House
With two thumbs raised high.

Hello, My Name is Mitch and I'm a Political Junkie

Who would have thought that Donald Trump, a thrice married, white 70-something New Yorker, multi-billion dollar real estate developer/investor and popular reality TV celebrity with no political or public service experience - nada, zilch, zero, gornicht - would be a few months away from capturing the American presidency and becoming " the most powerful man" in the world?

Truth be told, I did.

I sensed, when Donald Trump first announced he was running for the presidency in June of 2015, that he was going to crush all his Republican opponents and that he would ultimately and decisively defeat the Democrats' chosen flag bearer, Hillary Clinton.

Simply, Trump is the American people's revolutionary and populist reaction to the pathetically weak, politically correct reign of the Emperor King Barack (Barry) Hussein Obama II, the Chosen One. Chosen by and crowned by the LA/Chicago/Washington/New York liberal establishment political/finance/entertainment elites.

Trigger Warnings:

- If you worship at the liberal altar of "Diversity, Inclusion, Affirmative Action";
- If you believe CNN, *New York Times, Washington Post* and Anderson Cooper are the Gospel Truth;
- If you believe Islam is a peaceful religion and ISIS is just an extreme ideology that has nothing to do with Islam;
- If you suffer from micro-aggressions at the mere mention of such offensive terms as "radical Muslim terrorists";
- If you believe that "All Lives Matter" is racist. That in fact any criticism of black-on-black killings, Obama, Mexicans, Muslims, Palestinians or illegal migrants is racist;
- And if you believe that any criticism of lying, morally compromised, power-hungry, nearly indictable Hillary Clinton is sexist –

Then, poor brothers and sisters, this book is not for you!!! Put it down. Delete it from your laptop or smartphone. Go take a cleansing shower. Wipe this opening from your memory.

However, if you want insight into American political history in the making, and some understanding of the successful Making of The Donald as President, the Collapse of the Kenyan/American/Christian/Muslim Obama and the self-implosion of Hillary, the most mendacious candidate in American history, then join me on these following pages.

I warn you the ride will be wild, crazy, hysterical, offensive and totally nuts.

Some of you may fall by the way side.

But for those few of you - brave, courageous, freedom-loving rebels who passionately hate political correctness and the fracking American elites who believe they and they alone should run your lives...

You will discover with me American democratic politics at its purest and craziest, at its worst and its best.

PART TWO:

THE RACE TO THE WHITE HOUSE - PRIMARY SEASON

PART THREE:

AMERICA IN TURMOIL

PART FOUR

THE DEMOCRATIC AND GOP CONVENTIONS

President Obama and then his General Counsel in the White House.

The Exeter experience helped me gain acceptance to Harvard University in the early '70s, where I majored and graduated Bachelor of Arts, Cum Laude (Honours) in political science, aka Government at Harvard. In those days, I was an idealistic liberal Kennedy Democrat type, as were 90 per cent of my fellow classmates. As far as I can tell, 90 per cent of the class of Harvard-Radcliffe '74 to date are still hardcore Democrats.

Plus ca change, plus c'est la meme chose.

I still remember with fondness spending hours hanging out with fellow political animals and cradle-to-grave Liberal Democrats at the Kennedy Institute of Politics, usually with another close friend, also an Exeter classmate and a street smart Boston pol from birth. For many years this friend was heavily involved in Massachusetts Democratic politics. Most recently he served as key adviser to then-Democratic Governor Deval Patrick, the first African-American Governor of Massachusetts.

I then went on to do graduate work at the University of Toronto in international law which involved business law and constitutional law on both sides of the border. At Harvard and at University of Toronto, then as throughout my life, my focus and interests have been on American and Canadian politics and policies on all three levels of government.

At an early age in the 1960s I was weaned on the *New York Times*, at the time the most important and influential national American newspaper. The "newspaper of record."

My, how the mighty have fallen!

Being Jewish, the grandson of immigrants on my father's side, I have always had a passion for urban politics, ethnic politics, racial issues and immigration matters. Which will be relevant later in this book when I consider the candidacies of Trump and Hillary in the context of such hot button issues as their differing views of radical Muslim terrorists, immigrants both legal and illegal, Muslim immigrants, racism, prejudice and Black Lives Matter.

Speaking about colour, if President Obama is considered a man of colour, what are we white guys considered - men of no colour? Are we therefore simply colourless?

Personally, I have always thought of myself as a colourful personality. As to my skin tone, after a day at the beach or on the links, I tend to be more swarthy than a pinkish preppie WASPy hue.

As to white privilege? Yes, liberal guilty, as charged.

I am a product of a white privileged background.

But note that my father, son of Jewish/Yiddish-speaking Lithuanian immigrant parents in the dirty, anti-Semitic '30s of Toronto, did not consider himself a very privileged white guy. Prejudice, hatred, and anti-Semitism were rampant. Much like the situation for Jews in American cities of that time.

In those days in Toronto and in most Canadian cities, certain public establishments refused to serve Jewish people, as in "No dogs or Jews allowed" in this restaurant.

Many Canadian universities in those days had negative quotas against Jews. Literally the opposite of affirmative action for black people. More like negative deterrence for Jews.

In Toronto as in many Canadian and American cities, many businesses, banks, life insurance companies and even hospitals did not hire Jewish people on the basis of their religion.

My father, notwithstanding that he had worked his way through undergrad, Pharmacy school and then Med school, all at University of Toronto, often working several jobs at once, knew that the WASP and Catholic hospitals of Toronto were closed to him.

Simply because he was Jewish.

Fortunately, in those days, the Montreal Jewish community, being a generation older and more established (the majority of Jewish immigrants having landed in Montreal in the 1850s), combated anti-Semitism, especially relating to its Jewish doctors who had been denied admission to Montreal WASP and Catholic hospitals.

But did Jewish doctors stop traffic in the middle of highways, waving signs saying "Jewish Doctors' Professional Lives Matter"?

No, they did not. Instead, the Jewish community solved the problem of anti-Semitism in this context by digging deep within its own community. They organized, funded from their own resources and built their own Jewish community hospital for the community's growing Jewish community and as a place for Jewish doctors to practice medicine.

Hence my father Aubie, the ghetto kid from the mean streets of Toronto, found his way to Montreal's Jewish General Hospital and a new life.

What is often forgotten in the endless discussion of anti-black racism in the US is that just about every immigrant group - like the above-noted Jewish community that found its way to the United States - experienced prejudice. In the late 19th and early 20th century it was the Irish, the Italians and the Greeks. Later on in the century other ethnic and racial groups experienced societal and institutional prejudice due to color (Asians, South Asians, Japanese) or due to lack of English skills (Eastern Europeans, Vietnamese, Koreans, Persians, Latinos) or in the case of many such groups, both.

Yet for the most part, all these communities, including the majority of their members, sucked it up. Formed solid family units, worked their asses off, stressed educational achievement or at least grit, determination, sacrifice and ambition. And by and large, with the support of tight families and their respective communities, the second and third generation of these ethnic communities have thrived and prospered in the greater American society.

These communities did not fight racism or prejudice by blowing away white cops.

Or engaging in South Asian-on-South Asian killings (or Korean-on-Korean or Persian-on-Persian killings) while blaming American racism for inherent problems in their own particular societies.

All American ethnic communities matter. All American racial lives matter. All American lives matter.

One of the underlying themes of this collection of writings is the struggle of Americans to define themselves as Americans. What are American values? Is America a multicultural country where all foreign cultures and their values and beliefs are equal? Or is America a set of shared fundamental values and beliefs, which predominate over other values, beliefs and even religions which may offend and undermine those fundamental American values? Which leader best embodies the true values of Americans? Which leader is able to define true American values and defend America against values and belief systems that undermine true American values?

A few final personal points.

Political beliefs:

On Facebook, under relationship status, people often write "Complicated".

My political beliefs - also complicated.

Simply I am fiscally conservative on the right, but as to social issues and beliefs, I am very much left of the spectrum.

I am a descendant of Jewish people - a very visible (and often loud and argumentative) minority group; a tribe, a community that has been persecuted for centuries. Of course I am in favour of the disadvantaged and the underdog.

My father was a very well-known, caring and compassionate obstetrician and gynecologist, who taught me at an early age about the horrible consequences of back alley abortions and the adverse consequences arising out of ignorance about all matters sexual. So of course, I have always been pro-choice and pro-female reproductive rights.

Together with being pro-LGBTQ rights and obligations and same-sex marriages.

On a related topic, I pride myself on being a feminist, since birth. Whatever that means these days.

I was raised by feminists such as my grandmother and mother, two very tough, no nonsense and independent women who were both graduates of McGill University ('22 and '44 respectively.)

I married two feminists - that is, two high-powered corporate securities lawyers.

Not at the same time, of course. That would be illegal - at least in certain parts of the United States.

But maybe not in Michigan.

And I raised two feminist daughters, one a hard-driving Wall Street lawyer and the other a political science major, like her old man, and a very smart senior analyst in the current Liberal provincial government of Ontario.

And as a Canadian, my family, friends and I have personally benefited from a government-run, single payer, affordable, accessible and universal national medicare program.

So mark me down for government-run healthcare.

Now as to my politics...

A woman friend, whom has known me for decades, once asked me in frustration, "How can you, a seemingly intelligent guy from a liberal Jewish family who has voted Liberal for generations, and who has been educated at the finest and most elite American liberal institutions, ever want to associate - let alone write favorably about - American conservatives and, even worse, American Republicans?"

My friends, therein lies a whole other book.

But I will try to be brief.

This book is not only about me. It is also about The Donald and Barack and The Hillary.

Ironically, though I was born and raised a liberal, I started questioning liberalism and liberal Democrats while at Harvard, the heart of Kennedy liberalism, during my years there from 1970-74.

The United States during 1967-74 - just as in these current times - was going through some major changes. The government was pursuing an unpopular war in Vietnam and the country was heavily divided between anti-war opponents and the silent majority who were pro-military, pro-war and pro-America. The race riots of 1967 in Detroit, which expanded to other American cities, showed that there was still a great racial divide between black Americans and white Americans and within each group: Militant blacks versus moderate blacks and conservatives versus liberal whites.

Though the U.S. was going through some massive changes, the predominantly liberal student body at Harvard thought it was business as usual, and the solution was just larger government and more taxpayer money to throw at these very real national and urban problems.

At Harvard it became apparent to me that conventional liberal views and opinions comprised a certain rigid political orthodoxy in which it was understood that all Harvard students should follow. Which would come to be known as political correctness.

Though I was supposedly surrounded by the "best and the brightest" of American students, I found most of the undergraduate students sleepwalking through American politics, oblivious to the significant societal changes around them. These students were just content with voicing empty slogans. Liberal arrogance became a substitute for critical and creative thinking, at least in the political sphere.

Ironically, the dominant liberal democratic culture had become the establishment culture and the most rebellious outliers on campus and clearly the most interesting and provocative were the Young Republicans, the real campus political counterculture.

By the end of my four year Harvard undergraduate career, my feet were solidly planted in two camps; the fiscally conservative Republican side which was also populated by "the least government is the best government" laissez-faire capitalists, Libertarians and Ayn Rand types. And the camp which believed that "the state had no business in the bedrooms of the nation."

Subsequent to Harvard I did not become a "community organizer" like Obama and spend 20 years of my life in a church run by and listening to incendiary sermons by a flaming anti-white, anti-American black militant holy roller.

However, I did leave the shelter of the ivy league ivory towers and returned to Canada and threw myself into the nitty gritty of Conservative politics: Organizing, canvassing, political strategizing and fund-raising for a variety of provincial and federal Conservative politicians.

All the while keeping close tabs on American politics: The Carter years, the Reagan years, the Clinton years and, most recently, the Age of Obama. And taking the occasional shot at Obama in the *Huffington Post.*

In the last few years of the Obama era I sensed a greater divide in American society, not only between the upper income one per cent and the rest, but between the blue Democratic states and the red States, between black and white and Islamic and non-Islamic.

I also sensed a great divide between the American urban liberal professional elitist class on both coasts and the average working folk in the south and in the Midwest.

Being an elitist myself, I sensed the utter indifference and ignorance of my fellow urban elites to the problems of millions of Americans outside our little self-entitled and self-imposed, gated and golden enclaves.

I also sensed that Donald Trump, a self-made Queens multi-billionaire, intuited the growing gap between the classes in American society. And that as in Canada, the working classes had been abandoned by both the left and the right, leaving a political vacuum.

And Trump saw his once-in-a-political-lifetime moment to seize this political opportunity and ride this bucking bronco all the way to the White House.

On June 15, 2015, Trump publicly announced his run for the presidency, and the rest as you will read in the following pages, is American political history, folks!

PART ONE:

DONALD TRUMP- RUNNING FOR THE AMERICAN PRESIDENCY.

ARE YOU FRIGGIN KIDDING ME?

Before Trump There Was Rob Ford, Populist Mayor of Crazy Town

PREFACE: *For me, my understanding of Trump' s political success and my foreknowledge of Trump ultimately capturing the White House commenced with my covering the wild and crazy roller coaster-like populist success of the former mayor of Toronto, my friend Rob Ford, from his upset victory in 2010 to his untimely demise in 2016.*

Rob was both loved and hated.

He was a "crazy as a fox" public figure who had terrific political instincts and a very loyal and immovable base. But he also attracted visceral opposition from opposing politicians (mostly liberal and socialist city pols) together with an almost deranged enmity from the liberal mainstream press.

Does this sound familiar?

The incredible Ford story has Trumpian echoes. And vice versa.

The following piece (I wrote over 30 pieces for the Huffington Post *and* Canada Free Press *over a period of three years) on Ford is verbatim. I wrote it on November 11, 2013, after Ford had been in the Toronto mayor's office for three years, and after he had confessed to smoking crack cocaine.*

There are some policy differences and differences on the fringes between these two populist public figures.

But on the fundamentals Trump, like Ford, enjoys enormous populist support from millions of working class and middle income voters, regardless of race, color, creed, religion, gender, sexual preference and ethnicity.

Trump is just not the spokesman for a narrow group of angry, old white working class males. Trump represents millions and millions of Americans who are unhappy with the elites who purport to represent their interests and these millions of American voters want to change the existing status quo in Washington. (The same applies to Boris Johnson and the millions of Britons who voted Brexit and wanted to shake up the status quo by leaving the European Union and the insensitive, unelected and unaccountable EU bureaucratic elites.)

Also, Trump's political opponents (i.e. Hillary, the Democrats) and the elites on the left and right and the liberal mainstream press do not understand his appeal and who his real democratic base is, or why his expanding base is sticking to Trump, come hell or Whitewater.

Perhaps after reading this Ford article, you too will see why Trump and Trump's forces will crush Hillary this November in the presidential election.

The article, as it appeared in the Huffington Post:

Why Ford Is Still the Man to Beat

Apparently the reports of Rob Ford's political demise have been greatly exaggerated.

I thought that when Ford confessed to having smoked crack cocaine, he would be forced out undemocratically by Toronto City council or Ontario's Liberal Premier Wynne.

Four Toronto newspapers, including the *National Post* and *Toronto Sun*, all called for Ford to resign.

Ford was the butt of jokes on every late night American comedy show from Jon Stewart to David Letterman. Much to the mortification of some overly-sensitive Torontonians.

So Toronto's four great newspapers have collectively spoken. Ford must go.

But a funny thing happened on the way to the "powerful Toronto media" trying to ride Ford out of town on a GO Train rail.

As a result of these papers raging against Ford, his support increased by about 5 points to about 44 per cent approval.

I am not sure what is declining faster — these papers' circulation numbers or their rapidly declining influence on public affairs.

What is patently clear is that in these papers' rush to judgment, they don't understand Ford's populist appeal.

And long after their newspapers are used to line the city's cat litter pans, they still will not get it.

I think all those years of drinking fancy tea at Davids Tea, sipping Almond Milk at Whole Foods and eating organic beef from Rowe Farms - where everybody knows your cow's name - may be the cause.

I don't think even 30 days of rehab in Scarborough will do the trick.

But I will try one more time to explain the populist and enduring appeal of the Ford phenomenon.

I have known and met many members of Ford Nation in the last few years. I have met them at coffee shops, restaurants and in their homes. I have met them at Ford Fests.

The bulk of Ford's support is in the suburban cities outside of downtown Toronto, being Etobicoke, North York and Scarborough.

Many Ford supporters are hard-working lower-income and middle-income families who have immigrated to Toronto from all corners of the world: From Asia, South Asia, Africa, the Middle East, Eastern Europe and South America, just to name a few.

Rob Ford, the white WASPy guy from a wealthy business family, appeals to all these different peoples. He also appeals to a lot of old line white and ethnic Toronto families.

They love and support Rob Ford. Their support is deep, wide, visceral and unbreakable. They will stick by Ford even if he is convicted of a criminal offence.

At these Ford Fests, Ford is treated like a rock star. Ninety percent of his people are non-white. They have come to see Ford, not for the free beer and hot dogs. But to be photographed with Ford. To hear his simple message, of saving their tax dollars. And stopping thc "gravy train" of free-spending urban elites. And of course: "Subways, subways, subways!" The battle cry of these suburbanites who for too long had been ignored by the lefty Millerites at City Hall.

I have covered Canadian and American politics since the '70s. Ford's immigrant non-white supporters revere Ford as if he was a combination Bobby Kennedy, Bill Clinton and Barack Obama.

It has to be seen to be believed.

For some strange reason this Ford character relates to and understands these people. Ford understands that his supporters are worried about making their rental payments, their mortgage payments, buying groceries for their families and ensuring their children are properly educated. They are worried about their jobs and whether good jobs will be available for their children in the future.

They work very hard for their money, and they resent that their tax dollars, in the past, paid for unnecessary and very expensive vanity projects of Mayor David Miller and his left wing acolytes on council.

These people resented these councilors flying all over Canada and the world on their dime. They resented these councilors' over-inflated office budgets. They resented that Miller treated city hall as an employment agency for his union buddies. Miller's city hall granted union members jobs for life with overly expensive pensions. Such financial benefits were paid for by Ford's supporters on one hand, but were out of their reach on the other hand.

Ford supporters also resented that Mayor Miller and his lefty acolytes apparently spent most of their time and their taxpayer money, trying to "save the whales" - promoting and imposing policies these suburbanites believed were irrelevant to their own daily needs and wants. For example, a highly subsidized urban bike program, anti-car, city bike lane proposals, penalties on plastic bags, vegetable gardens on city's roofs - all to save the planet.

To his credit, Ford delivered on his campaign promises. During Ford's first three years in office, he gained control of the city budget. He reduced the rate of tax increases from Miller time. He tamed the unions and implemented the partial privatization of some garbage city services. He also drastically reduced his own mayor's office budget and the budgets of all 44 city councilors at considerable annual savings. And he scored an unusual political coup by securing tri-level financial support for the expansion of the much-needed and much-desired Scarborough subway.

Ironically, the full-on media onslaught against Ford, this over the top Ford hate-fest, has turned a mirror on his Old Toronto critics. And exposed them as elitist, self-centred, power-hungry, undemocratic, condescending, ignorant and insensitive.

Any politician who courts Ford's Old Toronto critics is no friend of Ford Nation.

Rob Ford will still be the person to beat in next year's municipal election.

June 17, 2015

Donald Trump Announces His Run for the Presidency at the Trump Tower.

Rubio and Bush Be Afraid - Be Very Afraid

* * * * * * * * * * * * *

Well, it's official: Donald Trump, the thrice-married real estate mogul/entrepreneur and popular reality TV host, has thrown his chapeau into the Republican ring.

And politics as we have known it - especially boring, staid, WASPy GOP politics - will never be the same.

I am not exactly sure what will happen, but this will not be a rerun of the boring, uptight Mittens Romney primaries.

This may be heresy, but I believe the Donald can beat all his lesser known GOP opponents.

First, none of these dudes have Trump's name recognition or star presence.

Trump has been in our faces for years. As a real estate mogul. Party boy. Man about town. Husband of three gorgeous women. Hotel guy. Casino guy. Art of the Dealmaker. And more recently as host of his own television reality show, which has been watched by millions. He is bombastic. Crude and rude. Funny. Egocentric. But he gets stuff done. That's a heck of lot more than you can say for these other boring career politicians.

On the other hand, there is Jeb Bush. The Jebster. He is the safe choice. The establishment choice. He is the Mitt Romney of this election.

Ironically, though he may be smarter than his older brother George W. Bush, he seems to lack his brother's humour, charm and popular appeal. Basically, he is not as likeable as Dubya. He is stiff. Quiet. He is not very natural or at ease in public. He looks uncomfortable in his own skin. And that may hurt him.

Jeb will probably have tons of money behind him but he is carrying the baggage of his brother's trillion dollar failed Iraq invasion/adventure. Also, in May of this year Jeb was in favor of the Iraq invasion before he was against it after three other tries to get the right answer.

What was Jeb thinking about for the last six months as he was exploring running for the presidency?

This is going to be the GOP's great white hope to beat Hillary? The down and dirty Clintons will steal Jeb's lunch money and hang him upside down in his locker for sport.

On the Iraq question - "Would you have done the same thing, knowing what we know now?" - clearly Jeb was caught between his loyalty to his brother, his own real views, Hillary's position, the other position of the candidates and what was the right and popular answer on the Iraq question.

Frankly, Jeb looked like a fool and, ironically, after all these years of planning for his run for the presidency, the Jebster is still not ready for prime time.

Trump's other main rival is Hispanic Marco Rubio from Florida.

Some GOP hotshots think Marco will attract much needed Hispanic voters to the GOP fold with his convoluted and complex immigration reform policies.

I am not sure if Marco is strong enough to withstand the fiercely conservative Senator Ted Cruz from Texas who is virulently anti-immigrant and anti-free choice and anti-gay.

So I see four main contenders: Jeb, Cruz, Marco and the Donald, the last thanks to simple name recognition and the novelty of a TV personality running for the president without any public or political experience.

At least TV host Ronald Reagan had a California governorship under his belt.

But on the other hand, GOP primaries are Hobbesian affairs: Short, brutish and nasty.

They are not for the faint-hearted or nuanced policy wonks, which the Jebster and Marco appear to be.

I have read Trump's populist speech several times.

Trump's points are simple, but very powerful.

1. Obama is a loser. Hillary is a loser. America's leaders are weak, hence America is a loser and weak.
2. Trump is a winner. Always been a winner. He will make America a winner again.
3. America has entered into bad trade deals with its opponents, i.e. China and Japan.
4. Valuable working class and middle income jobs have been lost.
5. The elites on the left and the right don't care about the working class or the middle class.
6. Trump will do better trade deals and bring back good jobs or prevent good jobs from going to Mexico.
7. Mexico is sending America its illegal dregs of society. Among them are criminals and rapists.
8. Islamic terrorists are being let into America and American leaders are not doing enough to keep America safe.

The mainstream press can laugh all they want at Trump. But in these complex and unsure and unsafe times, clear statements are needed.

I think Trump has tapped into working class angst.

Also Trump did not turn himself into an ideological pretzel by talking about divisive social issues as abortion and same-sex marriage and gay rights.

In the words of that wise southern Democratic old boy from the south, James Carville, Trump is talking about jobs, jobs and jobs. In other words: "It's the economy, stupid."

I think the Donald has a great shot.

August 17, 2015

The GOP Primaries - Post First Debate Analysis Trump Continues to Lead All the Other Losers

★ ★ ★ ★ ★ ★ ★ ★ ★ ★ ★ ★ ★

I am sure that when the Bushes - father, son Jeb and brother George - met to plan the succession to the Bush throne by Jeb the Younger, they never expected that court jester Sir Donald of Queens would be leading the polls in August, before the first GOP debate, by a good 10 points over his next opponent, the hapless and feckless Jeb.

(I hate a guy who lacks feck.)

So a quick recap as to the race for who will be the GOP presidential nominee:

Recall that around June 15, 2015 both Jeb Bush and Donald Trump announced their candidacies.

Conventional wisdom would have Jeb Bush as the leading GOP candidate in a normal election.

But this is not a normal election.

As of a day before the first GOP debate of August 6, 2015, among the ten most popular candidates, the dark horse with the unique hairstyle and youngish third wife, Donald Trump, is leading the pack with about 23 per cent, followed by Jeb Bush around 12 per cent and Scott Walker at about 10 per cent.

Leave it to Trump to turn lemons into lemonade. His weaknesses into political virtues.

Trump has no political experience and he is boastful of that lack of experience.

He brags that he is not a traditional politician. Because he creates jobs.

There is a certain populist logic to that statement.

In fact, Trump prides himself on being the political outsider, the one candidate truly running against the establishment.

Trump is running a very negative grievance campaign and it is apparently working.

Trump is saying to both the GOP and the Democratic leadership: A pox on both your houses.

You, the political establishment of both parties, don't know what you are doing. You are all losers.

Or worse, you know what you are doing. You are looking after yourselves and the people and companies who donate to your campaigns, greased by evil greedy lobbyists.

Bottom line: The American people. The people who have lost their homes as a result of the 2009 recession. Got the shaft. While the venal bankers who were bailed out by Washington politicians using American taxpayers' hard-earned money, skated scot-free.

Furthermore, good paying jobs in the Midwest of the country - in the heartland states of Illinois, Indiana, Iowa, Kansas, Michigan, Minnesota, Missouri, Nebraska, North Dakota, Ohio, South Dakota, and Wisconsin - were disappearing due to badly negotiated free trade deals which benefited America's trading partners and certain American financial elites on both coasts, but not the people most affected by factory closings.

By some strange twist of political fate Donald Trump, the wealthy New York real estate magnate, has tapped into some serious working class and middle income angst and anxiety.

And Trump alone seems to be speaking to these angry and unhappy and frustrated Americans, whose American Dream has never been realized

This view and Trump's name recognition and very large personality may explain in part Trump's unexpected lead prior to the first televised debate.

I watched the Fox News debate among the ten GOP contenders answering questions from Megyn Kelly and Chris Wallace.

Trump dominated the debate. He won handily and Jeb Bush and Scott Walker just wimped themselves out of the race.

Bush and Walker, second and third going into the debate - two Republican governors with cred and experience - got whipped by Trump, badly.

These two so-called experienced politicos just do not have a clue about how angry the GOP electorate is with Obama and with their lives.

They want a fighter. They want a shit disturber. Not two wimps.

To the GOP base, there is already a Wimp-in-Chief in the White House.

When Chris Wallace asked if all the candidates would pledge to accept the winning GOP nominee and not run as a third party candidate, Trump was the only one not to pledge. He showed some cojónes. He stood out.

He knows he has an independent following and the GOP need him more than he needs them.

That is exactly the type of hard-nosed leadership and attitude the GOP base wants, in reaction to the spineless leadership of Obama.

As Trump has done in the past - and especially in his opening campaign speech in June - he criticized Obama for entering into a bad deal with Iran. He also played to the base by complaining the politicians in Washington on both sides of the aisle have failed to close the Mexican borders to illegal aliens and that some of them are criminals and rapists.

Also Trump implied that illegal aliens were taking the hard-earned jobs of true blue Americans and legal immigrants.

In contrast, Scott Walker was too weak and accommodating.

And Jeb Bush started humming kumbaya. Jeb Bush completely misread the GOP base and in doing so, just lost his only chance to be the GOP nominee.

Bush tried to come across as the white Obama. He was against Trump's negativity and grievance campaign.

He thought America was stronger if everyone just got along and danced with flowers in their hair around the maypole.

(Okay, that last part was fiction, but you get the drift.)

The angry GOP base does not want Obama-like platitudes. They are angry and they want action.

Good-bye Walker and the Jebster.

You both are toast.

As for Bush the Younger, you just fired yourself!

Mission: Not accomplished!

As I surmised, after the first poll post-GOP debate, Trump's tough guy, strong arm tactics carried the day: Trump was up to 25 per cent, Carson up to 12 per cent, Ted Cruz up to 10 per cent, Jeb Bush dropped to 9 per cent and Walker dropped to 6 per cent.

November 1, 2015

Dowd of the *New York Times* Cuts Little Jeb Bush Down to Size

★ ★ ★ ★ ★ ★ ★ ★ ★ ★ ★ ★ ★

No one writes with such relish, caustic wit and insight than Maureen Dowd of the *New York Times,* especially when she psychoanalyzes the crazy psychodrama of the Bushes: Poppy Bush, Dubya, the wayward prodigal son, and Jeb, the heir apparent*.

Jeb was always the favored son in the eyes of his parents, and he was supposed to ascend to the Presidency. But Jeb's ex-alcoholic playboy brother George beat him to the White House and Dubya is getting the last laugh. It now appears Jeb is a horrible, boring campaigner and is getting taken to the cleaners by the outlandish, but very effective, Donald Trump.

Jeb has also been forced to defend the Iraq invasions of his older brother and, as Dowd opines, the Jebster has been unable to properly answer for his brother's actions. As a result, Jeb's candidacy is in the toilet. Say good-bye to the presidency, loser.

For all his faults, George W. Bush could connect with the people. He did win two presidential campaigns.

Jeb can barely connect with his own family.

* "Fall of the House of Bush", Maureen Dowd, *New York Times*, October 31, 2016

November 22, 2015

Douthat of the *New York Times* Sees GOP Field and Dreams of Richard Nixon

★ ★ ★ ★ ★ ★ ★ ★ ★ ★ ★ ★ ★

I urge you all to read Ross Douthat's excellent column today*. Douthat is the *New York Times*' token conservative commentator. He argues that we should ignore Nixon's Watergate fiasco and his paranoid personality and instead focus on the qualities that made him the successful political leader who decisively won the 1968 and 1972 presidential elections. Because it is these gifts that seem well-suited to the current situation.

Douthat writes that though Trump has successfully earned populist support from people who are worried about jobs, immigration, terrorism and an overreaching social liberalism, Trump is a provocateur who plays at being a bigot, and as a result there is a ceiling to his support. Nixon's genius, according to Douthat, was that he tapped into the same populist anxiety about social change and disorder without repudiating racial equality or civil rights. His was a more nuanced approach.

Similarly, Nixon had the gift of appealing to people's non-ideological character. He was a political pragmatist and opportunist. Nixon went wherever the voters he courted needed him to be. He was left of Goldwater and right of Rockefeller. In American terms, the GOP leader has to have the Nixonian ideological flexibility to restrain out-of-control federal government programs - i.e. Obamacare - in a stagnant economy, without shredding the safety net. In other words, the successful GOP candidate must show a flexibility greater than what GOP orthodoxy demands.

On the foreign policy front, Douthat once again argues for a multi-dimensional and cold-eyed Nixonion realpolitik approach, when he astutely states: "We don't face a single Soviet-style threat or a convenient 'axis' of allied evils. We can't defeat ISIS and contain Iran and push back Russia and restrain China all at once. So we need a president who can see the strategic chessboard whole, who can instill fear in our rivals but also negotiate boldly in situations where opportunity presents itself. And that sounds much closer to Nixonian realpolitik than it does to the full-spectrum hawkishness most Republicans are running on."

It is a brilliant piece and I also invite potential federal Conservative candidates for the leadership and their advisers and their supporters to check out this article, because it has relevance to them as well.

* "Searching for Richard Nixon," Ross Douthat, *New York Times*, Nov. 21, 2015

November 29, 2015

Dowd of the *New York Times* Channels her Angry Right Wingnut Brother and Hammers Obama and Hillary

★ ★ ★ ★ ★ ★ ★ ★ ★ ★ ★ ★ ★

I urge you to read a devastating take down of Obama and Hillary by Maureen Dowd's acerbic right wing brother in today's *New York Times**. Kevin Dowd's best hits against Obama include calling out Obama for "leading from behind," refusing to name the enemy as Radical Islam, stupidly calling ISIS "contained" before the ISIS Paris attacks, still calling Islam a religion of peace, refusing to insist on proper screening for Syrian refugees, sidelining himself and the US against the international war against ISIS, all while still maintaining the greatest threat to the world is climate change.

Kevin hammers Clinton for seeking the presidency when 60 per cent of Americans don't trust her and being under FBI investigation for emails that may have breached national security. Kevin concludes with three questions:

- Do you want a president who refuses to name the enemy?
- Who do you want to appoint the next three Supreme Court justices?
- And who will protect the homeland and honor the Constitution?

Kevin Dowd believes America has lost its way under Obama and Hillary.

Query: Has the failure of Obama/Hillary led to the creation of The Donald, as self-proclaimed savior of American greatness and exceptionalism?

* "King Kevin Versus Queen Cersei," Maureen Dowd, *New York Times*, November 26, 2015

December 15, 2015

Final 2015 GOP Debate - Snow White Trump and the Three Dwarfs: Dopey (Rubio), Sleepy (Bush) and Sleazy (Cruz)

* * * * * * * * * * * * *

This was the last debate of 2015. About six months ago both Trump and Bush announced their respective candidacies.

For six months, these two front runners have been heading in different political directions.

Trump ascending.

The Jebster dropping into the toilet.

"What's it all about, Alfie?"

Perhaps the times, they are a changing.

Ironically Trump, the political neophyte, is the one who possesses the acute political instincts. The ability to intuit who his base is and what they want. But also what the vast majority of Americans want, regardless of political leanings.

Whereas Jeb Bush, with the support of the GOP establishment and $100 million in the kitty from wealthy GOP donors, is completely clueless.

Perhaps Jeb thought he just had to show up at the debates, and with his political pedigree and experience, all opposition to him would fade.

Clearly, Bush has not counted on The Donald, who has developed a brilliant presence on social media, with over 5 million Twitter followers and a robust Facebook following.

What the mainstream liberal press and even the establishment right wing press do not appreciate about Trump is that in developing this social presence, Trump has been able to tap in directly to thousands - if not millions - of average Americans who not only receive Trump's tweets, but also respond in kind.

What Trump has done is cut out the middlemen of political advisers and go directly to the people to understand their desires, their needs, their wants, their fears and their hopes.

This is real and true politics in 2015. Whereas Jeb Bush (and even yesterday's woman, Hillary Clinton) is caught up in the politics of the pre-internet. Relying on fancy and highly paid sycophantic advisers, and costly and inaccurate focus groups.

Also Trump knows how to play the mainstream media beautifully.

He is such a provocateur and quotable character that major radio and TV news shows vie for his presence. Usually Trump just has to call up a TV news station to get on the air, securing valuable and free media exposure.

For Trump in this "dog eat dog" survival of the craziest and most outlandish primary season, there is no such thing as bad publicity.

This Trump dude is crazy like a fox.

Trump had the brilliant political instincts to sense that many Americans were concerned with the continuous influx of illegal immigrants into the United States, especially from Mexico.

But in the Age of Obama, it is politically incorrect to speak ill of such illegal immigrants.

So Trump has come up with the brilliant political plan of saying the unsayable.

Saying what a large number of people are thinking, but are afraid to say.

Like, "Mexico is sending a lot of bad people to the U.S. We are not getting their best. We are getting rapists."

Or: "The only way to stop the influx of these bad people is to build a wall to keep them out and Mexico will pay for the wall."

Hence the Trump catch phrase "Build That Wall" has become the rallying cry of Trump forces.

Such campaign slogans are Reaganesque in their simplicity, and also in their power.

As simple as Ronald Reagan's rallying cry to end the Cold War: "Mr. Gorbachev, tear down this wall."

Or when Reagan publicly referred to the Soviet Union as an "evil empire."

In the same vein, Trump has learned from his numerous social media interactions that a vast number of Americans are worried about the rise of ISIS, and more specifically they are worried about home grown radical Muslim terrorists within America's borders.

Almost daily Americans have been bombarded with online images of radical Muslim terrorists - killing, beheading, torturing and bombing innocent people in many parts of Europe and the Middle East.

Many Americans remember the 2009 Fort Hood massacre where a Muslim army doctor terrorist killed 13 Americans soldiers.

More recently, on July 16 of this year, a religious Muslim made a suicide attack at a recruiting and naval centre at a strip mall in Chattanooga, Tennessee, killing five people. On December 2nd, a radical Muslim terrorist couple attended a Christmas party in San Bernardino, California and shot fourteen people dead.

These were clear acts of terror by radical Muslim terrorists. Not mentally unbalanced lone wolf crazies as Obama and the Democrats and the mainstream, politically correct liberal press would like the American people to believe. Real live radical Muslim terrorists, bent on killing Americans in the service of Islam.

Accordingly, the American people are rightfully fearful of these random but premeditated acts of violence against them by religious adherents to a supposedly "religion of peace."

Trump hears, reads and feels their fear. Specifically, at a Trump rally in Las Vegas prior to the December 15 debate, Trump rightfully questioned how San Bernadino killer Tashfeen Malik was able to obtain a fiancée visa to enter into the United States when it was clear from her social media accounts that she was a radicalized Muslim.

Accordingly, Trump once again said the unsayable, and called for the temporary ban of all foreign Muslims into the United States until the American national security forces can figure out how to protect Americans from home grown radical Muslim terrorists within their borders.

Well, when Trump came out with this plan, the proverbial chop suey hit the fan.

Trump was criticized from both the left and the right. From the whole of the Democratic leadership - Obama all the way down.

As well as from the Republican leadership and Trump's opponents in this GOP presidential race.

I believe the more Trump says the unsayable, and the more politically incorrect he is, the more his support rises, while the more the clueless Jeb Bush opposes him, the more loser Bush types drop into the political toilet.

Prior to the December 15th debate, according to a recent poll, Trump stood at 41 per cent, while his nearest rival, Ted Cruz, was about 27 per cent behind at 14 per cent. Jeb Bush had dropped to single digits.

Jeb Bush's political and personal collapse has been absolutely stunning.

Despite his experience, the Bush name, his political infrastructure and the over $100 million he raised.

With about six to eight weeks to go until the first Iowa caucuses and the New Hampshire primary, I declare Jeb Bush dead in the water.

Brought down by hubris, pride, ignorance, arrogance and terribly weak debating performances.

Trump rightfully made fun of Jeb's low energy and listless performances.

Clearly this Bush lacks that fire in the belly; that determined will to win practically at all costs.

As to the December 15, debate itself, in many ways, it was anti-climatic.

Jeb Bush finally tried to get a few shots in at Trump, calling him the "chaos candidate," implying Trump was totally unfit for the sober responsible job of Commander-in-Chief.

And Bush was right for a change. Trump has become the chaos candidate. He is the great GOP establishment political disrupter.

Much the way Amazon and the internet have destroyed the video store and the record shop.

Bush lamely tried to call Trump out on being a racist for banning all Muslims to the US on the basis of religion.

But that battle had already been lost.

Trump nailed the fact that a large number of Americans have lost confidence in the Obama government protecting

Americans from radical Muslim terrorists, and that the GOP establishment is not that much better.

That is the underlying fear Trump knows and to which he responds in real time.

The other interesting development of this debate was the emergence of two potential rivals to Trump, the conservative, fire-breathing Christian evangelical Ted Cruz and the young Hispanic Marco Rubio from Florida, who is the last white/Hispanic hope of the GOP establishment.

The sweet irony of all these debates is that the supposedly more well-known and experienced Senators Cruz and Rubio need the exposure of these televised debates more than the political neophyte Trump.

Because of Trump's amazing access to social media and free TV and radio interviews at his whim.

By the end of December, 2015, Trump was trending at around 40 per cent, about double his nearest opponent Ted Cruz. And early polls on Iowa and New Hampshire are showing Trump ahead of Cruz.

Which is absolutely mind-boggling!

Recall that Trump is from very cosmopolitan, urbane, sophisticated and multicultural and multiracial New York.

In the past, Trump has been supportive of pro-choice, gay rights, single payer government-run health care and he has been thrice married.

Trump does not exactly embody your traditional Christian family values conservative Republican.

But he is leading in the heavily Christian, conservative family values Iowa caucus against Mr. Christian Evangelical himself, Senator Cruz.

Folks, there is a revolution in the making in the GOP.

Trump is leading without paying fealty and sucking up to the pro-life, anti-gay faction of the party.

Perhaps this is a come-to-Jesus moment for the socially conservative right in the GOP party. Perhaps jobs, jobs, jobs is more important to voters than being misled by the false promises of the false prophets of the Washington GOP establishment elite, and that the abolition of abortion isn't just around the corner. And that gay rights and same sex marriage and equal rights for all LGBTQ aren't just passing fads.

Wow!

I think the Donald has a very real shot to take the GOP nomination and go all the way and beat the over-rated and highly mendacious to her core, Hillary.

But before I double down and bet the farm on the Donald to go all the way to the golden Trump White House, I want to see first that Donald's support can translate into votes on the ground.

I am an old political organizer from way back.

The big question for me is: Can the Donald get his supporters out to the Iowa caucuses and the New Hampshire voting booths.

If he can, then the Donald - to paraphrase a Bushism - "is not all hat and no cattle."

If he can take New Hampshire, I believe in my political guts that The Donald is going all the way to the White House.

Whatever happens, it will be a wild and crazy ride in 2016!!!

December 15, 2015

Thomas Pynchon's *Inherent Vice* – A Subversive Attack on the Intrusive Obama Administration

* * * * * * * * * * * * *

(a film review)

*(**NOTE:** It is early in the primary season. The candidates for both the GOP and Democratic parties have been debating throughout the fall. The first primaries will be held in February, 2016. We are in full campaign swing.*

But something odd and strange is in the cultural air. I feel it. No, it is not the all female sequel to Ghostbusters.

I sense a part of Liberal-dominated Hollywood - the deeply conservative, libertarian part - is turning away from Obama and the heiress to the throne, Hillary.

Liberal Hollywood is typically very supportive of the Democratic President and it has been gaga to date over Obama.

But here is a film, penned in 2009, set in L.A. in the '70s, that is subtly and subversively very critical of the Obama government in 2009 and going forward. Its violation of individual rights and its inherent corruption.

Pynchon saw it. I see it. And I think many Americans are questioning the legality and morality of Obama and his government. Of course, when it comes to the Hillary, the American people long ago determined that she is an amoral, immoral, unethical, power-hungry career politician, who thinks she is above the law.)

Thomas Pynchon, one of America's finest living authors, is a well-known chronicler of the tragicomic dark side of American society, culture, and politics. His very funny and provocative book, *Inherent Vice*, was published in 2009, during the first two years of the Obama Administration.

I argue that *Inherent Vice*, though set in the groovy sex, drugs, and rock and roll scene of 1970s Los Angeles, should be viewed as a subtle yet sharp critique of President Obama and his administration.

Remember Obama's campaign promise of "Hope and Change"?

Obama promised to end polarization in America; to unite the blue and red states. To make America transcend the racial divide. And to restore people's confidence in the American government by reining in law enforcement authorities and the national security agencies, whose powers have grown exponentially since 9/11.

Pynchon has written extensively on government control and interference in the private lives of Americans. I think that within the first two years of the Obama Administration Pynchon realized Obama had no desire to regulate and restrict such government agencies. In response, *Inherent Vice* foreshadows Obama permitting American law enforcement and national security agencies to double down and spy upon the lives of millions of Americans via various modern technologies - especially members of those American groups who opposed Obama, his administration, and the Democratic Party.

Pynchon, through *Inherent Vice*, holds a mirror up to Obama and his administration for the apparent illegal actions of his government. The film, adapted for the screen and directed by Paul Thomas Anderson, faithfully captures Pynchon's ingenious reworking of the classic private eye noir film. It's part Philip Marlowe, part *Chinatown*, part Altman's *The Long Goodbye*, with a pervasive whiff of weed a la *The Big Lebowski.*

But at its core, the film is all Pynchon. It casts a deeply realistic and paranoiac view of excessive government power, the government's penchant for spying on its own people, and the system's corruption.

The hero is Larry "Doc" Sportello (Joaquin Phoenix), a thirty-something laid back hippie. He's a pot-smoking private investigator, a gumshoe (or, more appropriately, gum sandal) who lives and works in seedy south L.A., near Gordita Beach. Doc is everyman: He is a working stiff. He lives alone in an apartment near the beach and shares a simple office with a pill-dispensing doctor. Doc also wears a weird Afro and has huge, mutton-chop sideburns reminiscent of Neil Young in the CSNY/Crazy Horse era. Despite his appearance, Doc has a strong moral code. He is an individualist, street smart and resourceful. He is very loyal to friends and family, and often does his P.I. work pro bono. He is incorruptible. **And he is very cynical and wary about the federal authorities.**

To simplify a complex and many-layered plot, Doc is approached by Shasta, an ex-girlfriend. Once also a stoner chick, she has now apparently gone a bit upscale in order to search for her missing lover, a high-rolling multi-millionaire real estate mogul named Mickey Wolfmann. (No relation.) But then Shasta disappears and Doc embarks on a noble quest to find both Wolfmann and Shasta, for whom he still holds a torch (or more appropriately, a doobie.) Doc suspects the pair may have been kidnapped by The Golden Fang, which may be a shady Asian drug syndicate or a front for coke-snorting, tax-evading LA dentists.

Throughout the film, viewers learn that Wolfmann, a lapsed Jew, conversely and perversely surrounds himself for protection with anti-Semitic, neo-Nazi, Aryan biker-types who may or may not also be involved with supplying arms to local black militant, Nation of Islam ex-cons. They, in turn, are being stalked by a gun-toting white American vigilante group. The vigilantes are working together with the neo-Nazis, and may or may not be outsourced, private contract killers for the federal government. (Got all that?)

To further complicate matters, Doc is also retained by a young mother, Hope, also a recovering heroin addict. Hope has a young daughter and believes her husband, Coy Harlingen (Owen Wilson), a drug addict and saxophonist allegedly dead due to overdose, may in fact still be alive and hiding in plain sight as an informant for the FBI … or some other shadowy federal national security agency.

Notwithstanding this panoply of psychotic sociopaths, the real villains of this film (according to Pynchon and Anderson), may be the Feds themselves. They are portrayed as the puppet masters, pulling strings behind the scenes. They are the FBI and Homeland Security; strait-laced, clean-cut, God-fearing, black suited, crew-cut, Mormon types. And they appear to be behind the infiltration of civil rights, black, and other dissident groups; kidnappings of prominent businessmen; contract killings of LAPD detectives and leaders of non-conforming groups; and the apparent development, sale, and distribution of illegal street drugs.

Though *Inherent Vice* is, at face value, a wacky sex and drug-infused fiction, it hits dangerously close to home … especially to the White House and President Obama.

As citizens we have learned, through the revelations of former security analyst and contractor Edward Snowden, that the national security forces under Obama monitor our phone conversations, texts, and emails. And that's not just Americans, but the phone conversations, texts, and emails of foreign leaders, too. Those we count as both friends and foes.

Under Obama, these same national security forces have infiltrated - through electronic wire-tapping and surveillance, and on-the-ground informants - many local American groups. That is, not only local Muslim groups but also Tea Party groups, Republicans, media groups and any other political and community groups opposed to Obama and the Democrats.

Add to that the serious allegations that the independent Internal Revenue Service has been compromised by the Obama Administration into auditing, for political purposes, charitable and non-profit groups including the Tea Party, Republicans, and other conservative and anti-Obama PAC groups. Their link? All seem opposed to Obama's political agenda.

Note the very words of the title. "Inherent Vice" is a legal concept which implies that the thing itself contains the seeds of its own destruction.

I highly recommend Pynchon's *Inherent Vice*, both the book and film, because it reflects Pynchon's prescient observation that the Obama Presidency, at its outset, contained the seeds of its own destruction.

How wonderfully ironic that Hollywood, one of Obama's most solid bases, would in turn expose the inherent vice of his Presidency.

January 6, 2016

Trump Calls Hillary Sexist for Enabling Slick Willy's Willy

★ ★ ★ ★ ★ ★ ★ ★ ★ ★ ★ ★ ★

Recently, Hillary Clinton criticized Donald Trump for allegedly making sexist comments. Instead of publicly censoring himself like most spineless white male politicians, Trump lashed out at Hillary and publicly stated what millions of Americans have been privately thinking for years.

That Hillary, the self-proclaimed great white hope of American womankind, had stood by while her philandering horndog of a husband, both as Arkansas governor and as president, preyed on vulnerable women (Paula Jones, Juanita Broaddrick, Eileen Wellstone, Monica Lewinsky and who knows how many more), seduced them, used them, abused them and then publicly humiliated them.

In effect, Hillary had enabled Bill Clinton to commit crimes far worse than Trump allegedly uttering sexist comments. So why didn't Hillary dump Bill's sorry ass? I have my theories, and hope to address that burning question later.

How ironic would it be if Hillary's run for the presidency is ultimately thwarted by her being hoisted on Bill Clinton's own petard - or peckertard, as the case may be?

PART TWO:

THE RACE TO THE WHITE HOUSE

PRIMARY SEASON
TRUMP VS. 16 LOSERS

FALTERING HILLARY "FEELS THE BERN" FROM BERNIE

February 10, 2016

Why New Hampshire Voters Flocked to "Let's Make America Great Again" Trump and the Wild-Eyed Socialist Sanders

New Hampshire voters handed stunning victories to the two outsiders: Donald Trump and Bernie Sanders.

Donald Trump won 36 per cent of the GOP vote, followed by Kasich at 16 per cent. Then the three also-ran amigos: Canadian-born Ted Cruz, Jeb Bush and robotic Mario Rubio, all at 11 per cent.

On the Democratic side, Vermont Senator Bernie Sanders humiliated Hillary Clinton by defeating her 60 per cent to 39 per cent.

I love the fact that the majority of so-called political experts and pundits on both the left and right in the US and Canada are stumped by the success of the Trumpster and the raging septuagenarian socialistic Sanders, the junior senator from small town-state Vermont.

Trump's reality TV show run for the presidency was supposed to have fizzled months ago. The experts had the GOP coalescing behind the heavily-funded and favored Jeb Bush or the more immigrant-friendly, youthful and telegenic Marco Rubio.

Except, unlike Trump, none of these other candidates appear comfortable in their own skins.

Jebster will never be ready for prime time. In the debates, he came across as boring and indecisive, burdened by his tight-assed New England upbringing and the collective memory of his brother George's shoot-from-the-hip, overly militaristic and economically unsustainable presidency.

Meanwhile, Rubio is just a poor man's middle of the road Cuban Mitt Romney, caught in the vortex of the GOP's highly primal primary politics. In the most recent New Hampshire debate, Rubio shot himself in both feet as he robotically repeated his talking points. One day Rubio is all for legitimizing the illegal immigrants. The next day, bowing to the anti-immigrant GOP right wing, he is all for deporting them.

In this sense, he and the other Republican contenders are much like the now reviled President Barack Obama.

President Barry started with such "hope" and promise, but he has been exposed as the sorriest US president in the last century. He talks - and talks and talks - but on the world stage he carries a very limp stick.

Barry, the leader of the most powerful country in the world, is openly mocked by the thuggish Putin, Arab oil sheiks and Iranian mullahs, to whom he continually prostrates himself. He constantly seeks their approval, just as he unsuccessfully sought, throughout his life, the approval of his distant Kenyan father, who had abandoned him at an early age.

Obama will be forever associated with the pussy-whipped slogan, "leading from behind." His disappearing "red line in the Mideast sand on Syria," was the final straw that broke the camel's back (to mix Mideast metaphors.)

From that time forth, Putin jumped in and overshadowed him. The Iranian mullahs mocked him. And Barry's key allies in Europe, the Mideast (Israel), Asia (Japan) and South Asia (India) began distancing themselves from him and America.

The result?

An embarrassing near-fatal blow to America's confidence and national self-esteem, both domestically and internationally.

On the domestic front, the economy has benefited the wealthy on Wall Street and Silicon Valley, but the middle class of Middle America? Not so much. And these angry Americans blame Obama and the political elites from both parties for their financially stagnant lives.

All this accounts for the rise of both Trump and Sanders.

Americans - young, old, white, male, female and of color - want America to be great again. They are tired of settling for mediocrity. Of just getting by. They want to prosper. They want a better financial and economic future for themselves and their children. They want to have a shot at what Trump has - and is promising.

They want to live in a stronger and more competitive America which is not afraid to beat China, Japan and Germany on the economic front. A nation that is not afraid to stand up for American values both at home and abroad, one that will exercise its military power against its enemies.

As for the Democrats, Sanders genuinely believes that government can be a force for good and can uplift all Americans, beyond mediocrity to greatness. Sanders has captured the youth vote (both male and female) with his call for massive change. For a revolution: Free public college tuition. Universal, single-payer, publicly-run, affordable, government-controlled health care. That is, the Canadian Model.

And like Trump, Sanders has attacked the Wall Street and Silicon Valley elites who appear to be prospering at the expense of hard-working average Americans.

The big story in New Hampshire and in these primaries in general is that Democratic men and women under forty-five are flocking to Sanders and have abandoned the Hillary, and for many good reasons.

These young and middle-aged Democrats see Clinton as "yesterday's woman," a tired, old, fat congenital liar and prevaricator. Scandals, lies and deceptions are embedded in her DNA: Whitewater; Benghazi; the destruction of her national security/private emails; Slick Willy selling access to Secretary of State Hillary for millions - the list goes on.

Young Democratic women also see Clinton as no advocate for women's rights. Instead they view her as a power-hungry Lady Macbeth who humiliated and destroyed scores of vulnerable women who'd been victimized by her sexual predator of a husband.

I predict a Trump/Sanders fight to the death.

And a Trump White House in 2017.

February 21, 2016

Trump Steamrolls Over Politically Dead Ted and #Never Trump

The Trump for the Presidency train is leaving the station. Either the Republican Elites get on board, or look even more irrelevant and politically inept than they do now.

First there was mama's boy Jeb Jr.'s $100 million down the tubes. His campaign was the biggest and most expensive bomb in political history, the *Heaven's Gate* of bad presidential campaigns. Then the boring Ohio governor Kasich. Not a ripple of support. Good-bye, Columbus. Lastly, the Great Not-So-White Cuban Hope, Marco Rubio. Still not ready to play with the big boys.

In this post, I want to explain how Trump will lead the Republicans against either Clinton or Sanders. Cruz is dead in the water after South Carolina. He was cruising for a Trump bruising. And Rubio, of the silly repetitive talking points, lacks Trump's killer and acute political instincts. Marco-Polo-itically dead. RIP MP.

The results are in from the most recent Republican primary in South Carolina. As predicted, Donald Trump, won his second consecutive primary contest. Trump polled 32 per cent and the runners up - Senator Cruz and Rubio – trailed far behind with about 22 per cent.

I hate to the bearer of bad news to the Republican political establishment, the "Anyone But Trump" cabal of fat cat fossilized old fogies. Those die-hard denizens of the *National Review* and the *Weekly Standard.* The sanctimonious keepers of the conservative flame. And, of course, those hundreds of wealthy and well-connected long time conservative politicos who have been backing Jeb Bush and Marco Rubio.

But it is time to face the music and dance with Trump. Because Trump is going all the way in these Republican primaries. Whether you myopic political hacks are on board or not.

And the more you bury your collective heads in the political sands or tear your Brooks Brothers threads in frustration and hunt around for the anti-Trump - no name Kacish or not-ready-for-prime-time Rubio - you further continue to marginalize yourselves and call into question your previously hard-earned good political judgment.

Despite being attacked from all sides in the debates, despite multi-million dollar attack ads from Bush-supporting PACs, and despite being attacked by many lamestream media columnists and commentators from the *Washington*

Post, New York Times, the New Yorker, CNN and Fox News, Trump and his core support have held firm.

We have seen this populist movie before here in good old Toronto, with Rob Ford and then his brother Doug.

I predict that Trump's populist appeal is deeply emotional, visceral, personal and unshakeable. As broad as it is deep.

And his growing core supporters will stick with Trump through hell and high water.

The Donald's critics can call Trump all kinds of names until they are blue and red in the face - bigot, racist, homophobe, sexist, anti-immigrant, Islamophobic - but they have had no impact on him. More importantly, these epithets, this juvenile name-calling, have had no impact on Trump's core support, and will have no effect on this core group going forward into the spring, summer and fall, through the Republican primaries. And through the down and dirty winner-take-all race to the Presidency.

Nothing short of Trump being criminally indicted, will stop this powerful, seemingly indestructible Trump train.

After three hard-fought and contentious primaries in Iowa, New Hampshire, and South Carolina, we have a much better handle on who constitutes Trump's core supporters.

The most recent South Carolina primary confirmed that Trump had retained the support of men, moderate conservatives, those without college degrees and older voters.

In addition - and this was a huge shock to Cruz supporters and mainstream Republicans - Trump also won the support of white evangelical voters by 8 percentage points over Senator Cruz.

This very powerful and influential Republican group in South Carolina made up approximately 70 percent of Republican voters in the state and had been the backbone of Senator Ted Cruz's support. Obviously, no longer.

Recall about a month ago, in an effort to bolster his support among socially conservative Republicans, while at the same time alienating Trump from this very same group, Cruz accused Trump of "embodying New York values."

In other words, contrary to Republican socially conservative dogma, Trump was soft on abortion and gay marriage. Cruz further accused Trump, as a born and bred New Yorker, of being overly focused on money and the media.

Well, Senator Cruz - Duh!!! Donald Trump owes his very political and public appeal to being totally focused on success, money and the media. And Republicans - both social conservatives and moderates - appear to be fine with this, and are not too fussed about Trump not being extremely, flamingly anti-abortionist or anti-gay.

Because Republicans, young and old, male and female, conservative and moderate, urban, suburban and rural, all appear to more concerned about the economy, the threat of terrorism and radical Islam (both foreign and abroad), America's broken immigration system, and the fact that America has lost its way.

And Trump, above all the other Republican contenders, has clearly tapped into these issues.

My view is that if Cruz could not beat Trump in evangelical South Carolina, then I don't like Cruz's chances in delegate-rich and socially conservative states like Texas, Virginia and Florida.

Cruz's chances become even worse as the primary fight shifts to more moderate Republican states in the northeast, midwest and the west.

In addition, as Cruz falters more, I predict that Cruz's natural conservative support will gravitate to Trump, followed by the remnants of Jeb Bush and Kasich supporters, and not to the wishy-washy Rubio, who has clearly failed to inspire and connect with the greater Republican electorate.

To me, Trump's victory in the Republican primaries seems inevitable. To the clueless, Republican political establishment – not so much.

February 24, 2016

After Nevada, Hillary is Toast - Trump is Going all the Way

★ ★ ★ ★ ★ ★ ★ ★ ★ ★ ★ ★ ★

Last night, Trump won overwhelmingly in the GOP Nevada caucuses.

To date Trump has won in northeast New Hampshire, South Carolina, and now the wild west of Nevada. His support is clearly national and he is attracting all segments of society, not just angry old men and women.

Trump even captured 45 per cent of the Hispanic vote in the Nevada caucus, notwithstanding his strong anti-immigrant position.

(He also did very well in Iowa, coming a strong second to Cruz.)

In his victory speech last night, The Trump confirmed what I have been stating for weeks. Trump is winning the old, the young, the highly educated and as Trump so characteristically called them, "the poorly educated." To which he ad libbed, "I love the poorly educated. They are the smartest and the most loyal." That is pure Trumpism. Brilliant. Honest.

And that is why Trump is winning. He is connecting with people, like no one else in the Republican or Democratic races. Because Trump is being Trump: Profane, crude, blunt, brash, controversial. Anti-establishment. And the American people love him.

Sixty per cent of people polled in Nevada support a candidate who is not part of the political establishment.

I suspect that is true of Democrats and independents as well in America.

American people are sick and tired of both the Democratic and Republican establishments.

They are equally sick and tired of the very tired and disappointing Obama presidency. A president who is now being mocked and ridiculed in Europe, Asia, the Mideast and around the world for being a spineless wimp. For "leading from behind." For failing to step up when Syria's Assad crossed Obama's "red line," and for cutting and running in Benghazi and leaving Americans to be tortured and slaughtered. And for alienating America's closest allies: Britain, France, Germany, Canada, Japan and Israel and its Mideast allies, Egypt, Jordan and Saudi Arabia.

Obama has also diminished America and Americans in the eyes of its enemies; Russia, Iran and China, by Obama's inactivity, his indifference and his overall weakness and spinelessness.

And who has the politically tone-deaf Hillary Clinton aligned herself with, but the failed and failing Obama presidency.

Hillary Clinton epitomizes the American political establishment. The old, decaying and dying sclerotic status quo.

There is a revolution stirring in American politics. The angry American people are mad as hell and they are not taking it any more. And by electing Trump president they want to send a message to Hillary that will be heard around the world:

Get the frack out of Washington and politics, you tired, old, lying, corrupt, political hack!

February 29, 2016

Going into Super Tuesday, Christie's Endorsement of Trump is "Yuuuge!"

Poor Marco Rubio. Just when he thought he got his mojo back after landing a few solid blows against Trump in the last debate, he was blindsided by none other than the Jersey Brawler, Republican Governor Chris Christie, who came out swinging for his new BFF, the Trumpster.

Christie, a former presidential candidate, is one member of the Republican establishment who is leaping aboard the Trump Super Train that's hurtling out of the station, bound for overwhelming victory in the southern states on Super Tuesday.

According to Christie, he threw his support behind Trump because he viewed Trump as a strong leader, the only one who could take on the probable Democratic nominee, Hellfire Hillary Clinton, the Arkansas Krusher.

As Christie astutely noted, the Clintons don't want to see the Trumpster in the ring. They "do not know the playbook of Donald Trump because he is rewriting the playbook."

Conventional wisdom was that in order to win in these complicated Republican primaries, a candidate needed thousands of volunteers in the trenches, getting out the vote, a tactic known as a ground game.

Also in the past, successful candidates required the support of local Republican bigwigs and grand poobahs, plus tons of moolah from special interests, to make huge negative advertising buys.

Trump had neither a ground game nor the support of local GOP notables. Also, Trump's campaign is mostly self-financed, so he does not owe favours to any filthy special interest groups.

Nonetheless, Trump smoked the competition in the New Hampshire and South Carolina primaries and he is going to run roughshod over his opponents in the southern conservative states on Super Tuesday.

The Donald has become the master of the traditional media as well as social media.

His anti-establishment message is resonating with young and old, male and female, white and of color, blue collar workers, professionals and business people.

Accordingly, Republican majority leader Kevin McCarthy from California is now on side, together with a growing number of no-name Congressional Republicans.

Even Nikki Haley, Republican Governor of South Carolina, and a public supporter of Rubio, has publicly admitted that if The Donald is the Republican nominee, she will be able to work with him.

And therein lies Trump's trump card: Winning. In politics, winning is everything.

Poor Marco Rubio doesn't get it. He is still coming across as a weak, frightened and clueless little Bambi, caught in Trump's oncoming headlights.

Rubio's latest fallback position is that even if The Donald wins the nomination, Republicans will not vote for him. Basically, Rubio is saying: I may be a loser, but I am a preferred loser. So vote for me anyways.

Of course, Republicans will vote for Trump in the general election, likely in greater numbers than they voted for the boring and uninspiring Mitt Romney during the last presidential rodeo.

Republicans, like Democrats, are in politics to win, not to hand over victory to their arch enemy - in this case, the hated Clintons - without a fight.

Remember, Republicans are mad as hell at the Obama Democrats. They do not want a white female clone of Obama, in the guise of the Hillary.

What I also find "yugely" amusing is the juvenile responses by some GOP operatives to Christie's endorsement of Trump, as reported by *Politico*:

> *Tim Miller, Jeb Bush's former spokesman, lit up Twitter with cutting comments. "Like Trump, Chris Christie is a pathetic, corrupt man with a tiny ego. I'm sure they bonded discussing their insecurities over a big meal," he tweeted.*
>
> *Bush strategist David Kochel also laced into Christie. "New lesson kids: sometimes, the best option for the fat kid is to just hand his lunch money over to the bully! #TrumpChristie2016," he said on Twitter."*

Recall that Miller and Kochel were part of the Jeb Bush campaign brain trust that blew through $130 million with nothing to show for all that hard-earned American cheddar. These two so-called political pros were part of the most expensive and worst campaign in primary history, a political debacle of Titanic proportions.

If I was either one of those bozos, I would be hiding my head in shame, probably on some obscure beach in Ibiza. The last thing I would be opining on would be the political acumen of any politician.

But these old political hacks are like their candidate: A pathetic, sore and clueless loser who had no business playing with the big boys and girls.

I predict that when Hillary comes up against the hard-charging and disruptive Trump juggernaut, she too will suffer the same political fate as the sorry Jeb Bush.

March 2, 2016

David Brooks of the *New York Times* Makes a Complete Fool of Himself on PBS Over Trump

* * * * * * * * * * * * *

I just love watching these stuffed shirt pundits, be they liberals or conservatives, make utter asses of themselves. So-called conservative pundit David Brooks of the *New York Times* embarrassed himself and his newspaper on national television last night during Super Tuesday.

The numbers do not lie: Trump won eight major states decisively from Massachusetts and Vermont to Virginia and then Alabama and Arkansas. He was a solid second in Texas, Cruz's home state and Oklahoma, neighbor to Texas. And in Alaska, he came in a very strong second. Trump only badly lost in Minnesota, coming in third to Rubio's only win.

But Trump's popular support was overwhelming.

Chuck Todd on NBC and Amy Walters on PBS analyzed the numbers and both concluded Trump is bringing out huge numbers of Republicans in larger numbers than in previous primaries. Trump is appealing to all demographics. They both concluded that he is the change candidate. And he is swamping Hillary in overall appeal.

Trump will be the GOP nominee.

Yet pundits like Brooks just can't bring himself to admit this. In the face of cold-hearted facts and numbers.

Brooks is hoping against hope the GOP leaders and the officials will rally around some unnamed anti-Trump.

But Cruz shot his bolt on Super Tuesday. He does not have strong support outside the conservative evangelical south.

And Rubio is a pathetic lightweight. He has come in third in all these states except he did win Minnesota. Woop-dee-doo!

Rubio is done and I predict that Rubio will lose to Trump in Florida. That will be Rubio's Waterloo as well as the endgame for all those GOP leaders who are deluding themselves into thinking they can stop Trump and his widespread and overwhelming popular appeal.

The more the GOP leaders talk about trying to stop the populist Trump with his huge popular support, the stupider and more out-of-touch they look. Trump has made them into political idiots, just as he has done with nearly every liberal and conservative pundit.

I read all these left-wing and right-wing pundits, from Remnick in *the New Yorker* to Brooks of the *New York Times* to Eugene Robinson of the *Washington Post* and my Harvard classmate Bill Kristol of *The Weekly Standard.* All these pundits have put their ideology ahead of clear and objective analysis. They are also the big losers in this Trump-dominated election.

I love the smell of conservative and liberal ideological blindness and ignorance in the morning. Especially so-called pundits such as David Brooks, whose ideological blinkers have blinded him to the Trump train that is running over his reputation and the reputation of all those other so-called pundits and experts.

March 3, 2016

Elitist and Failed GOP Prez Candidate Mitt Romney Just Propelled Trump into the White House

On Thursday, Mitt Romney came out with a public condemnation of Donald Trump in an effort to stop him from winning the GOP nomination.

This is the same man who, during the 2012 presidential campaign, publicly badmouthed 47 per cent of the American electorate and dismissed them as useless parasites who did not pay taxes; who lived off the government, supported Obama and would never vote Romney. He said, basically, that they should be dismissed as garbage.

Ironically this very same 47 per cent of the population, many of whom are hard-working average Americans, are supporting the candidacy of Donald Trump. These very same Americans believe that the political and financial elites of America - the Clintons and the Romneys and their wealthy Wall Street and Silicon Valley supporters - have abandoned these people. Accordingly, they are attracted to Trump, who rails against these elites.

For the GOP establishment and Trump's opponents to look to Romney for salvation is the height of political stupidity and folly.

Here is what Romney said about 47 per cent of Americans in the last election:

> *There are 47 percent of the people who will vote for the president no matter what. All right, there are 47 percent who are with him, who are dependent upon government, who believe that they are victims, who believe the government has a responsibility to care for them, who believe that they are entitled to health care, to food, to housing, to you-name-it. That's entitlement. And the government should give it to them. And they will vote for this president no matter what … These are people who pay no income tax ..."[M]y job is is not to worry about those people. I'll never convince them they should take personal responsibility and care for their lives.*

Note that when he was confronted with the tape and video of this incredibly stupid public statement, Romney first denied its existence, then misstated it, then claimed it was taken out of context. He never apologized or took personal responsibility for this YUGE political blunder.

Mr. Romney should have shown this spirit and toughness four years ago, when he was competing against Obama for the presidency.

Romney is not only a few months late in this 2016 campaign, he is several years too late in showing some backbone.

Time to return to Utah, Mr. Romney, and to the dustbin of history. You are a two-time loser. And if you thought you were so superior to Trump, why didn't you have the guts to compete with him in this presidential campaign instead of taking futile shots from the peanut gallery?

March 6, 2016

The Sunday *New York Trump Times:* It's All About Trump

✶ ✶ ✶ ✶ ✶ ✶ ✶ ✶ ✶ ✶ ✶ ✶ ✶

My prediction is that, for the first time since 1984 (with Reagan vs. Mondale), a Republican presidential candidate - some unknown non-politico named Donald Trump - will beat Hillary in her own home state of New York. A recent New York Post poll has Trump shockingly ahead of Hillary in a head-to-head matchup. If Hillary loses New York, one of the bedrocks of the Democratic Party in the Electoral College, it is curtains for Clinton.

But Trump beating Hillary makes perfect sense. The very liberal and Democratic *New York Times* is a case in point.

Hillary just won some states on Super Saturday, yet the Times' three major Sunday columnists just devoted all their articles to The Donald. No wonder his numbers are rising in New York and around the US.

The liberal Nick Kristof* predictably views Trump as the devil incarnate. He's the most dangerous man in the world if he is elected president, according to certain neocon national security experts.

More interestingly, Maureen Dowd** condemns not Trump but his detractors, the very same neocon national security analysts who whine that Trump will be an international disaster. Dowd pointedly remarks that these very same Trump antagonists were the ones who convinced George Bush to invade Iraq and try to remodel Iraq in America's democratic image. This resulted in the loss of a huge amount of American life, countless trillions of hard-earned American dollars and the loss of American prestige throughout the world.

Dowd also smashes Romney for having the chutzpah and unmitigated gall to criticize Trump's candidacy when Romney himself lost a presidential election that he should have won, because Romney was a completely inept phony.

In defense of Trump, Dowd states somewhat admiringly that Trump genuinely enjoys campaigning and connecting with his crowds. As opposed to Hillary who views dealing with the public as a nuisance. Also, Trump-as-President is very believable when he states that he will look forward to sitting down and negotiating with Congressional Democrats over domestic legislation. Something that Obama never did in all of his 8 years of being president.

Dowd's article is a must-read.

From another perspective the *New York Times* conservative columnist Ross Douthat*** writes somewhat positively and cynically on those factions which are apparently supporting Trump. They are a mixed bag of evangelicals, secular moderates, white working class Americans, Wall Street supply-siders and anti-immigration populists, with party people, political opportunists and inevitabilists thrown in. (I fall within the last category, being a self-proclaimed pundit, who writes about the inevitability of Trump's presidency, both out of genuine belief and a desire to stir up shit.)

With all this coverage on Trump from the die-hard liberal *New York Times*, no wonder New Yorkers are moving into the Trump camp, as is the rest of the country.

Trump More Years!!!

* "Donald the Dangerous," Nicholas Kristof, *New York Times*, March 5, 2016
** "Chickens, Home to Roost," Maureen Dowd, *New York Times*, March 5, 2016
*** "The Elements of Trumpism," Ross Douthat, *New York Times*, March 5, 2016

March 7, 2016

I Don't Think Donald Trump Can Even Stop Donald Trump

✶ ✶ ✶ ✶ ✶ ✶ ✶ ✶ ✶ ✶ ✶ ✶ ✶

We still haven't seen the depths of stupidity to which Marco Rubio and the GOP elites (Mitch McConnell, Paul Ryan, Bill Kristol, Mitt Romney and Karl Rove) will descend as they cut off their noses, limbs and manhood to spite themselves and their own GOP party - all to stop The Donald.

At this stage of the political game, I don't think Donald Trump can even stop Donald Trump and his date with destiny: A duel to the death with Hurricane Hillary, the Arkansas Hellcat.

Recently, political analyst Ed Kilgore of *New York* magazine argued that it is not Trump and his massive ego that's threatening a takeover of the GOP - it is Rubio, and the politically tone-deaf GOP establishment who support his failing campaign.

The more Rubio loses, the louder he argues that he is the true voice of the GOP party and its elites. But to date he has lost badly in almost every important GOP primary by huge margins to Trump and Cruz, and is even 15 percent behind in the most recent Florida poll - his own home state! So who is the con man now?

And yet, Rubio and the elites are threatening to take the fight to stop Trump to the convention floor.

In other words, against the obvious democratic will of the people, they want to stop Trump in some brokered, behind closed doors sleazy deal.

Can these so-called GOP experts and fat cat politicos be any more stupid?

These idiots have just handed Trump an even greater cause:

The popular will of the people against the slimy back room machinations of power-hungry Washington insiders!

Bernie Sanders is right: There's a revolution going on.

It is the revolution of the people against the political elites. Trump is the agent of this change. Establishment figures will be drowned under this tsunami of anger.

This includes Hillary, the archetypal Washington insider, because the majority of the American people don't give a shite that Hillary will be the first female president.

You heard it here first. Trump is going to ride this wave of anger and revolution right into the Trump White House.

March 9, 2016

Aloha, Cruz and Rubio - Trump Kills in Hawaii, Michigan and Mississippi Primaries

★ ★ ★ ★ ★ ★ ★ ★ ★ ★ ★ ★ ★

Despite a full week of attacks from his rivals, and notwithstanding over $38 million worth of attack ads leveled against him, The Donald scored a huge win in Mississippi.

He also crushed Kasich, Cruz and Rubio in Michigan, America's blue collar heartland. Then in the early morning, he also won in Obama's supposed American birthplace, Hawaii. "Book em, Donald!"

In Mississippi, Trump beat Cruz among evangelicals (that's Cruz's firewall) and among those GOP voters who are anti-government, the latter by a two-to-one margin. In Michigan, Trump destroyed Kasich, his nearest opponent, and won the vast support of both men and women, GOP and Democrats, who have lost their jobs due to globalization and international trade deals.

In other words, the Reagan Democrats - those Democrats who crossed party lines to vote in Republican

Ronald Reagan - are coming back to the GOP fold for the first time in decades, due to Donald Trump railing against free trade deals.

And folks, this is one of the major reasons for Trump's unbelievable success to date. On every campaign stop, Trump has been hammering against free trade.

Contrary to the ignorant pundits in the mainstream media, Trump is winning, not because he is appealing to the base instincts of the American electorate. He is winning because he understands and is articulating the anger of millions of white and black Americans, who have lost their jobs and their homes to unfair international trade deals, which they believe have closed American factories and exported these jobs out of the United States.

Trump is winning on substance - on the economy and the economic injustice that a majority of Americans are experiencing.

Trump is also killing it in the media. He truly enjoys the spotlight and he is loving this campaign. And the more his critics attack him and blow millions of dollars in negative ads, the stronger he gets.

CNN analyst Van Jones has compared Trump to Sebastian Shaw, an X-Men villain: The harder you hit that character, the stronger he becomes.

In response to political buffoon Mittens Romney questioning Trump's business acumen, Trump flipped the proverbial finger at all his detractors. Trump taunted them by holding his election night victory news conference at the Trump National Golf Club in Jupiter, Florida - and catered it with Trump Wines, Trump Water and Trump Steaks.

Pure media genius!

March 12, 2016

Violent Hillary/Sanders Agitators Prevent Trump Speaking in Chicago

★ ★ ★ ★ ★ ★ ★ ★ ★ ★ ★ ★ ★

How are violent agitators, bent on preventing Donald Trump from speaking at a peaceful rally in Chicago, Trump's fault?

Simple answer, this is not Trump's fault.

Let us call a spade a spade.

The fault lies with those violent agitators who publicly stated that they wanted to shut the Trump speech and rally down. These violent individuals - and I would not even honor them by calling them protesters - clearly identified themselves as Bernie Sanders' supporters and Clinton supporters. In other words, they are leftists and Democratic supporters.

But of course, the liberal media and Trump haters will blame Trump for the actions of these people, who believe that they and they alone have the democratic and constitutional right to freedom of expression and freedom of assembly. But these agitators believe that any person or group who does not share their views or espouse views that they oppose do not possess and deserve similar democratic and constitutional rights.

Interestingly, this violent shut down of a peaceful Trump rally played out in Chicago. And it is not a stretch to suggest that the perpetrators of these violent, undemocratic actions were also staunch supporters of President Obama.

Accordingly, they are the face of the Age of Obama, which is fortunately coming to a close.

This is a President who campaigned on bringing the various groups of American society together.

But Obama, during his two terms, subtly stoked the flames of division in American society.

During his two terms it became commonplace and acceptable for left-oriented student groups to violently shut down peaceful public talks by political leaders or public commentators on American college campuses who did not share the agitators' beliefs.

Obama, the so-called great leader and great orator. Who stood by silently when the rights of American students were trampled by these violent perps.

The responsibility for shutting down Trump's talk at the University of Illinois is clearly the fault and responsibility of the perpetrators. And Obama, for his negligence throughout his two terms, should also bear responsibility.

Because these people who prefer violence to dialogue are his supporters. They are his people.

Shame on Obama. Shame on these people. By their actions, they are trampling on the American Constitution.

Lastly, and to his credit, Trump - when faced with a very difficult situation and not of his doing - acted calmly and responsibly under pressure and made the right decision to cancel his talk. Trump showed great grace under pressure.

And came across as cool, calm, contemplative, decisive and, above all, Presidential.

March 15, 2016

Whiskey Tango Foxtrot: A Very Pro American Military Film

★ ★ ★ ★ ★ ★ ★ ★ ★ ★ ★ ★ ★

(a film review)

*(**NOTE:** In the midst of these GOP primaries I was reading on conservative blogs and seeing in Trump rallies a resurgence of good old fashioned American patriotism. Trump's speeches to very enthusiastic crowds are usually punctuated with cheers of "USA, USA". American flags are very prominent. There is much flag waving.*

These crowds are uniformly very pro-American military; clearly Trump senses this and is definitely appealing to these Americans' sense of country and pride in their military.

The tragic events of Benghazi are discussed frequently in the conservative blogs and at Trump rallies. In a sense there appears a clear shift away from Obama's anti-war and apparently anti-military approach, at least among certain segments of the American population.

The feeling on the ground and I suspect throughout the country at least among pro-military and patriotic Americans is that Obama and Hillary let down the four men who died in the American compound in Bengahzi on September 11, 2012. And that the two of them lied about and blamed an anti-Muslim video for causing the invasion of the compound and the ultimate deaths of U.S. Ambassador to Libya Stephens and three other U.S. officials.

When in fact the invasion of the compound was as a result of a well-planned al Qaeda operation, timed to celebrate the infamous 9/11.

Clearly responding to this pro military shift in the country and potentially anti-Obama and anti-Hillary sentiment, Hollywood producer Michael Bay produced a very effective film about the Benghazi events, released in January 2016, called 13 Hours: The Secret Soldiers of Benghazi.

In this film, Bay made four points critical of Obama and then Secretary Hillary Clinton:

1) *Obama/Hillary had not provided sufficient security to Stephens and his men.*
2) *When the compound was under attack, Ob/Hill did not send in troops or air cover in an attempt to protect or save these men.*
3) *There is a strong suggestion that nearby American forces were told to stand down and not intervene.*
4) *Ob/Hill lied about the immediate cause of this*

> *invasion. The film depicted a well-planned al Qaeda invasion, not a spontaneous attack arising out of an anti-Islamic video.*

I was thinking of this background when I attended the Afghan pro military film Whiskey Tango Foxtrot *in March of 2016.*

This film should be viewed as a companion piece to 13 Hours.

The film also shows the American military in a good light, in sharp contrast to the reality of Obama and Hillary who appear both uninterested, disinterested and in the case of Benghazi, apparently negligent.)

Let me cut to the chase.

I thoroughly enjoyed this film. Precisely for the reasons that it has received mixed reviews from the liberal Hollywood press.

This is not an absurdist, anti-war film like *Catch 22*, based on Joseph Heller's classic World War Two novel of the same name.

Nor is this film an anti-war satirical film like *M.A.S.H.*, which took place during the Korean War (but was really about Vietnam.)

Nor is this a lame, unfunny, anti-American and anti-military, Michael Moore-produced piece of celluloid crap like *Where to Invade Next.*

Instead *Whiskey Tango Foxtrot* is a sympathetic comic/dramatic depiction of America's fighting men and women and the flawed sex/ booze/drug and combat-addicted male and female journalists who embedded with them in Kabul, during the Afghanistan War from 2003-2006.

This film, produced by Lorne Michaels of Saturday Night Live fame and star Tina Fey *(SNL, 30 Rock),* is loosely based on *The Taliban Shuffle: Strange Days in Afghanistan and Pakistan,* the Afghanistan war memoirs of former Chicago Tribune and now *New York Times* investigative reporter Kim Barker.

Tina Fey plays Kim Baker, a lowly copy writer on a no-name cable network based in New York. She's in a dead end job writing about the evils of fructose. She is also locked in a passionless relationship with a depressive boyfriend (Josh Charles) who is never in town.

Baker is given the chance to change her life and become a foreign war correspondent in Kabul, Afghanistan, reporting from the field.

Liz Lemon goes to Kabul, essentially.

Like her *30 Rock* character, Fey plays a nerdy, workaholic with a mediocre social life in New York.

But in crazy Kabul her new frenemy, fellow journalist Tanya (the beautiful Margot Robbie from *Wolf of Wall Street* and *The Big Short*) explains that whereas Baker may be a "6" in New York, she is a solid "9 ½" in Kabul, due to the absence of any western women in the field.

Accordingly, plain Jane Kim spends a good deal of time fending off the sexual advances, of Nic (Steven Peacocke), her New Zealand bodyguard, Iain (Martin Freeman), a randy Scottish photojournalist, and a local Afghan public official Ali Massoud Sadiq (Alfred Molina.)

Tina Fey is once again sharp, funny, feisty, tough and, independent. Her comic timing - bang on. As Baker, she is also initially clueless about the cultural complexities of an American female journalist in female-unfriendly Islamic Kabul.

Baker naively lets her hijab uncover her hair and is called a shameless whore by a female Muslim in the streets of Kabul. She loses her American dollars to the wind. She is scammed by a young beggar. And she is nearly beaten by an angry Muslim mob, when she is caught filming a group of men in an area where women are clearly prohibited.

Fortunately for Fey/Baker, she is often saved and protected in Kabul by local driver, fixer and translator Fahim, played skillfully with quiet strength and intelligence by a bearded, heavyset and unrecognizable Christopher Abbott (indecisive Charlie, Marnie's boyfriend in the hit HBO series *Girls*.)

Though the cultural differences are immense, by the end of the film they bridge the cultural divide and Baker and Fahim forge a friendship of mutual respect. Their final separation, as Baker returns to New York for good, is touching - literally and figuratively.

While embedded with the Marines on an exploratory mission "outside the wire" - that is, outside America's walled off compound - a fire fight ensues between the Americans and the Taliban forces. At great risk to herself, Baker throws herself in harm's way to film the fire fight.

A few things happen in Afghanistan for Baker. She loves the adrenaline rush of combat, and she earns some respect from tough Marine colonel Hollanek (played wonderfully by Billy Bob Thornton.) Hollanek also warns Baker that though she may be a "4" in New York, she is a "10" here. And therefore no distracting his men by shagging them.

As the film unfolds we watch Baker gain confidence through quick cuts of her on air, reporting confidently about various battles and developments in and around Kabul by day, then partying hard in the frat-house like compound for ex pat journalists, by night. Where there is nightly sex, drugs and rock and roll. Hooya!!!

What was memorable for me was how effectively the film puts Baker into difficult and delicate situations as a woman in a male-dominated war and a strictly male-dominated Islamic society, and how Fey/Baker adroitly navigates herself in these situations, and learns and reports on these situations.

In one scene, Baker is approached by a group of village women completely covered from head to toe, including their faces, who inform her that they, not the Taliban, are blowing up the wells built by the Marines so that they can go to the river to fetch water, as it's the only place they can freely talk and gossip away from the harsh restrictions imposed upon them by the mullahs of the village. Baker wins kudos from the colonel for that valuable intel.

In another funny but touching scene, Baker must in turn wear a full blue chador, which she jokingly refers to as to being encased in a full blue Ikea bag, in order to travel to the more dangerous Taliban-controlled city of Kandahar.

Where she witnesses and reports first-hand on a fire-bombed school for young women.

Compared to the Academy Award-winning film Spotlight, I liked the way the film depicts these war-hardened journalists and photo-journalists more honestly, as flawed human beings - motivated by ego, ambition and apparently addicted to seeking greater risks and dangers, often at the expense of those around them.

Finally, kudos to Fey, Michaels, the writer Robert Carlock, directors Glen Ficarra, John Requa and of course, Kim Barker for having the guts to bring the story of the forgotten war of Afghanistan onto the screen and to America.

Fortunately, the Age of Obama is coming to a close. It was a sorry time in American history, when America's fighting forces were ignored as a nuisance, instead of being honored for their service to their country. But the pendulum is swinging back. Above all, this film honors America's fighting men and women in far off wars.

Men and women who fight and put their lives at risk so that, among other things, Afghan girls can get an education and American men and women might be protected from vicious and evil radical Islamists as ISIS.

Hooya!!!

March 30, 2016

#NeverTrump Bill Kristol, my old Harvard Classmate = Disastrously Wrong about Trump

★ ★ ★ ★ ★ ★ ★ ★ ★ ★ ★ ★ ★

Ever since Donald Trump started winning Republican primaries, Bill Kristol and his fellow travelers on *The Weekly Standard* have written numerous anti-Trump tirades. But the more they fulminate against Trump, the more Trump keeps winning.

It's been enormously amusing to watch these GOP fat cat pundits humiliate themselves day after day, week after week.

They don't get Trump. They don't understand his populist appeal. They don't know or understand the millions of average working class Americans who are supporting Trump.

They also don't realize that their time has passed.

Within a decade they've gone from being powerful Bush advisers and neo-confidantes to political dinosaurs.

Instead of focusing his efforts on defeating the scandal-riddled, mendacious Hillary Clinton, Kristol and his right wing lunatic lackeys are trying to devise anti-democratic schemes to wrest the nomination from Trump in a brokered GOP convention.

And if that ridiculous effort fails *(ya think?)* Kristol says he wants to engineer the creation of an independent third-party candidate specifically to hurt Trump's chances of winning the presidency.

Bill, as your former Harvard classmate, I must confess that I did admire on occasion your political courage as a young Republican in a predominantly liberal/democratic Ivy League school. And since then you have certainly made a name for yourself as an influential conservative pundit and commentator.

But Bill, are you friggin' *nuts*?

There is no way in hell that Trump delegates at the GOP convention will leave their man behind after the first ballot and vote for some Washington-based GOP establishment political hack like Paul Ryan, or a clueless, politically tone-deaf Mitt Romney parachuted in to supposedly save the day.

Trump's populist support is rock-solid, primal, visceral and emotional. This support is reminiscent of the rock-solid and immovable support that Rob Ford enjoyed, despite (because of?) the over the top, often irrational media opposition, both nationwide and worldwide.

Now Kristol has floated the ridiculous trial balloon of encouraging some idiot to run as a independent third party candidate, a la Ross Perot. He approached the clueless former Texas governor Rick Perry who, to his credit, turned Kristol down.

Trump has gone on Sunday talk shows and criticized this move as a recipe for GOP disaster and a scheme that will guarantee the election of the hated Hillary.

Fortunately, the Republican National Committee, seeing the writing on the wall, has condemned Kristol's third party scheme as one that would just help Hillary.

Perhaps Trump supporters should take some comfort that Kristol has had a horrible track record of making disastrous predictions. In 2008, he predicted Barack Obama would lose every primary to Hillary Clinton. In October 2015, he predicted Vice President Biden would jump into the presidential race. Kristol was also convinced in February, 2016, that Rubio would win the New Hampshire Primary.

Kristol also has wrongly predicted on eleven different occasions that Trump had peaked! Yet the Republican establishment in Washington still takes Kristol seriously.

As an anti-establishment shit disturber at heart, I love the sight of puffed up, over-rated, conservative and liberal pundits, being hoist on their own petards.

I predict Trump will be the Republican presidential nominee and he will destroy Hillary in the general election. He will drive a stake into that cold, heartless, conniving, manipulative, untrustworthy woman, once and for all.

Trump more years.

April 27, 2016

Trump Krushes Krazy Kasich/Kruz Koalition

✶ ✶ ✶ ✶ ✶ ✶ ✶ ✶ ✶ ✶ ✶ ✶ ✶

Donald Trump has just experienced his most super of Super Tuesdays. On Tuesday night, he crushed his opponents - the smarmy Cruz and the inept Kasich - by overwhelming margins in Pennsylvania, Delaware, Maryland, Connecticut and Rhode Island.

To date Trump has secured 988 pledged delegates. His magic number now is 249. (He needs 1237 delegates to win the Republican nomination).

Trump is expected to win handily in such upcoming states as New Jersey, West Virginia and California.

The very liberal CNN, clearly no supporter of Trump, believes he will lock up the nomination in California, well before the GOP convention.

In other words, there will be no contested GOP convention, where the establishment Republican forces, in cahoots with the once reviled Cruz, would have used sleazy backroom tricks to frustrate the democratic wishes of millions of primary voters.

Most establishment political pundits at the *Washington Post, New York Times, The Weekly Standard,* CNN and Fox News have been saying ad nauseam that Trump will lose out to Cruz or some other establishment figure in a contested convention.

So what has changed in the last two weeks?

Well, Trump got his mojo back. He killed his opponents last Tuesday in his home state of New York, winning by healthy majorities throughout the state.

Then Trump took on the ridiculous attempt by Cruz and Kasich to gang up against him. Trump publicly lambasted his opponents for "colluding" together, a word that implies illegality. This was a typically over the top Trumpian attack, but effective nonetheless.

Trump also pointed out that such coalitions are terrible ideas both politically and optically. For liberal-oriented Kasich to jump in bed with extremely right wing Cruz, Trump insisted, demonstrates that neither man has any principles.

When reporters questioned Kasich about the coalition, Kasich tried lamely to pass off this major political development as "no big deal," and just a way to conserve his resources.

Say what? By telling his liberal supporters in Indiana and in Los Angeles to support the viciously right wing Cruz? Has Kasich gone completely nuts?

Then Kasich backtracked and encouraged his supporters to vote for him in Indiana after all. That will split the anti-Trump vote and definitely ensure a Trump victory in the Hoosier state.

Months ago, my political instincts suggested Trump would take the GOP primaries. Now the hard, cold numbers support this view.

May 4, 2016

Evangelical Indiana Came to Jesus for Trump over Cruz

★ ★ ★ ★ ★ ★ ★ ★ ★ ★ ★ ★ ★

As predicted, the Indiana Republican voters handed Donald Trump an overwhelming victory on Tuesday. Trump demolished Cruz 53 per cent to 36 per cent with the hapless Kasich getting only a pathetic 7 per cent of the vote.

Cruz has suspended his campaign. Trump now has a clear path to sewing up the GOP nomination for President.

Indiana was supposed to be Ted Cruz's fire wall, the state that was going to stop the Trump train in its tracks. A resounding victory in Indiana may have provided Cruz with the opportunity to beat Donald Trump in a contested GOP convention on the second or third ballot.

Note that over 50 per cent of the GOP electorate in Indiana are white evangelicals. These are Cruz's peeps!

And Cruz secured the endorsement of conservative Republican governor, Mike Pence, reputedly a hero of the religious right.

So where did Cruz go wrong?

Firstly, Cruz fatally misread the Indiana electorate.

In the last few weeks, Cruz had hammered Trump as being soft on religious liberty on behalf of the Christian right. In other words, Trump was pro-gay, pro-same sex marriage, pro-LGBTQ rights - especially the right of transgender people to use the washroom of their choice - and the right of gay couples to get wedding cakes from Christian bakers.

Cruz failed to realize that although Indiana is a conservative state, neither the evangelicals nor the Tea Party types have significant influence over the state's politics.

Indiana Republicans adhere more to Main Street values: Small business, small conservative government, without the emphasis on social conservatism.

Secondly, the evangelical voters in Indiana appear to be choosing Trump over Cruz and Kasich on economic and national security issues. That's what Republican evangelicals did in Mississippi, where 84 per cent of the GOP voters self-identified as evangelicals. In that primary, Trump won 48 to 39 per cent of the evangelicals. Trump beat Cruz among evangelicals in South Carolina by 33 to 27 per cent.

Note that even Indiana Governor Pence's endorsement of Cruz appeared lukewarm. In fact, he almost sounded like he was endorsing Trump:

> *I particularly want to commend Donald Trump, who I think has given voice to the frustration of millions of working Americans with a lack of progress in Washington, D.C. And I'm also particularly grateful that Donald Trump has taken a strong stand for Hoosier jobs when we saw jobs in the Carrier company abruptly leaving Indiana not for another state but for Mexico. (...) I'm grateful for his voice in the national debate.*

Frankly, that was one of the strongest, most thoughtful and most genuine comments in favour of Trump by any government official during these primaries.

Third, Cruz's coalition gambit with Kasich also hurt his Indiana campaign.

A recent poll concluded that about 60 per cent of the Indiana voters were opposed to the Cruz/Kasich coalition, the terms of which stipulated that Kasich supporters were encouraged to support Cruz in Indiana. Except Kasich supporters were sticking with Kasich - note his 13 per cent support in a recent *WSJ*/NBC poll.

I believe that Indiana voters rejected Cruz in part because this ridiculous coalition idea reeked of sleazy backroom politics, with the sole goal of stopping Trump, and not advancing any policies of interest to Indiana voters.

Lastly, for those Trump critics who are still deluded into thinking that Trump is a buffoon and a joke, he has pulled off an incredible political upset.

He beat Senator Ted Cruz in the heart of socially conservative, evangelical Indiana, by being his own guy and sticking to his strong economic message in favour of hard-working and middle income groups, while still supporting gender and sexual equality.

Note Trump specifically did not pander to the extreme right wing social conservatives of the GOP.

Accordingly, unlike Romney before him, Trump will be able to pivot to the centre without socially conservative baggage, and take on Hillary where she is weakest: improving the economy for the working and middle income groups.

Hillary, you should be scared. Be very scared of The Donald.

May 16, 2016

Shocking News! Hillary Feels Trump's "Bern" as Trump Surges Past Hillary

* * * * * * * * * * * * *

As I predicted in February when Trump won the New Hampshire Republican primary, Trump went on to take the GOP nomination. OK, I also said Bernie Sanders would take down Hillary Clinton before the Democratic convention. But I stand by my belief that Trump will destroy Clinton in the general election for president.

I have also been writing for months that Clinton is toast. The polls are finally catching up with me.

After months of head-to-head polls, in which Clinton had a double-digit lead over Trump, a recent Quinnipiac poll had Trump tied with Clinton in the two crucial swing states of Florida and Pennsylvania.

The same poll saw Trump besting Clinton 43-39 in the bell weather state of Ohio. Note that no presidential candidate has won the presidency since 1960 without winning at least two of these three critical states.

Predictably, Clinton's highly paid spin doctors quickly

dismiss this poll as an anomaly, put out by an outlier polling group.

That is, until the following day, when the better known Reuters-Ipsos group published roughly the same result. But this poll had Trump virtually tied with the stumbling Hillary, nationwide!

But the best poll was yet to come, showing Trump leading by 10 points against Clinton with Hispanics.

According to this Gravis Marketing poll, Trump's populist economics, which appeal to working class white Americans, is also resonating with Hispanics who are just as concerned about bread and butter issues. They don't like the idea of illegal immigrants taking their jobs, either!

Before the New York primary, Trump seemed stuck at under 35 per cent support, among supposedly angry white American working class men and women.

But after the New York primary gave Trump a majority, it became clear that his support was widespread and broad-based: Young and senior, women and men, urban and suburban. He garnered support from key Hispanic and ethnic groups as well.

Then Trump won decisive majorities in the nearby northeastern states of New Jersey, Connecticut and Delaware, and beat Cruz for good in the conservative evangelical state of Indiana.

With no remaining opposition, Trump romped to victory in the West Virginia primary.

All this time, Clinton has been stumbling badly.

She is a terrible and unlikable campaigner. The more people see and hear her speak, the more people are turned off.

In March in Ohio, Clinton blundered terribly. In an attempt to suck up to climate change eco interests, she bragged insensitively that she would, "put a lot of coal miners and coal businesses out of business."

Well, in May those comments came back to bite her in the posterior in West Virginia coal country. Sanders beat Clinton badly, while other Democrats crossed party lines to vote for Trump.

Typically, Clinton refused to properly apologize for those comments, citing that they'd been taken "out of context".

The fact is that for the last few months, Hillary has been getting beaten by a 70-something socialist, forced to fight Sanders from her left and Trump from the right.

The GOP establishment is grudgingly unifying behind Trump because many Republicans hate Hillary more, and his numbers are clearly improving.

My political instincts tell me that even the above polls are behind the curve.

I believe Trump is leading Clinton now by more than 10 points.

And I predict that even her last remaining fire wall - that of black men and women - will fall.

May 18, 2016

Clinton Campaign in Deep Deep Trouble after Less than Super Tuesday

✶ ✶ ✶ ✶ ✶ ✶ ✶ ✶ ✶ ✶ ✶ ✶ ✶

Last week Hillary Clinton and Bernie Sanders competed head to head in the Kentucky and Oregon Democratic primaries.

Kentucky, the Bluegrass State, was supposed to be Sanders' Waterloo. The septuagenarian Jewish senator from the small northeastern state of Vermont was supposed to be closed out by the formidable Clinton machine.

But Clinton failed to close the deal. Hillary barely squeaked by with a victory, beating Sanders 46.8 per cent to 46.3 per cent with fewer than 2000 voters out of a total of eligible and registered Democratic voters of 423,000.

Yes, Clinton won. But context is everything in this closely-fought primary battle.

Recall that the state of Kentucky has always been friendly to the Clintons.

Bill Clinton won Kentucky twice in his two presidential campaigns in 1992 and 1996.

In the 2008 Democratic primary, Hillary beat the then Senator Obama by 35 per cent of the vote or about by 250,000.

But this time, notwithstanding Hillary headlining eleven separate events in the last few weeks of the campaign, with her campaign making a significant financial investment in state-wide advertising and a last minute media blitz, Hillary just barely bested Sanders.

Even in victory, Hillary and her supporters were feeling "the Bern."

White working class Democratic voters, both male and female, largely rejected Clinton and voted for Sanders over Clinton.

Clinton was seriously hurt by insensitive comments she had made in Ohio in that state's April primary.

Recall that Clinton told a predominantly pro-green energy Democratic crowd in a CNN town hall meeting that her green energy program would put a lot of coal mines, coal mine owners and coal miners out of business. Those comments were widely reported in West Virginia and contributed to her loss there. And clearly hurt Hillary in the Kentucky primary.

Sanders really "Berned" Hillary badly in Oregon - 54 per cent to 44 per cent. Sanders won 35 of the 36 counties. He beat Hillary by 51,000 votes stateside. Sanders and his supporters simply outworked, out-hustled and out-organized the Clinton forces.

The Sanders team registered many young voters and then successfully got them out to vote.

As a result of the close Kentucky vote, Clinton and Sanders both won 26 delegates. And three remained to be decided.

In Oregon, Sanders won 31 delegates and Clinton 20 delegates, with 10 remaining delegates to be allocated.

As of May 20, 2016, Clinton has 2,289 delegates, 1,768 of whom are pledged and 521 are super delegates. Sanders has 1,522 delegates, including 1,481 pledged delegates and 41 super delegates. A total of 2,383 delegates are needed to win the Democratic nomination for president.

Clinton is just 106 delegates away from victory. But Sanders is not quitting.

Sanders has publicly stated that he will continue to fight Hillary right through California, the last primary, to the floor of the July Democratic convention in Philadelphia.

Sanders wants to use his popular support to significantly influence the Democratic policy platform going forward in the general election, and he and his fervent supporters want justice for his supporters whom Sanders believes have not been treated fairly and equitably by the Democratic powers that be, who seemed to owe their allegiance to the Hillary.

Blood may be spilled both within and without the Democratic convention.

I predict it will not be pretty and such division will prevent Hillary from quickly unifying the party against Trump in the fall months leading to Election Day.

May 26, 2016

WTF? Trump Captures GOP Nomination ahead of Super Tuesday
GOP Elites Collectively Suffer from PTSD (Post Trump Success Disorder)

* * * * * * * * * * * * *

It seems just a month ago that Senator Ted Cruz was "cruisin for a bruisin" with his opponent the Trumpster in a projected contested GOP convention in Cleveland in July.

In April, the Washington-based Republican establishment was hot to trot to trip up Trump. They were apparently lining up behind Ted Cruz in an effort to stop Trump on the second or third ballots.

Then came the May 3 Indiana primary. Trump crushed Cruz once and for all in that heavily conservative state (53.3 to 36.6 per cent). In fact, that was Cruz's last stand. He folded like a cheap suit after that ignominious defeat, followed quickly by one-state wonder Kasich.

Prospects of a contested convention vanished, together with any hope that Republican Trump haters would withstand the Trump juggernaut to total victory.

As of today, Trump has unofficially captured the GOP nomination for president.

The Associated Press delegate count has Trump reaching 1,238 committed delegates, the magic number being 1,237.

Several previously unbound GOP delegates have told AP that they would support Trump at the national convention, the most prominent and most visible being Oklahoma GOP chairwoman Pam Pollard.

Pollard has publicly stated in Trump's defense that, "I think he has touched a part of our electorate that doesn't like where our country is," Pollard said. "I have no problem supporting Mr. Trump."

In view of Trump's recent public squabble with New Mexico Republican Governor Susana Martinez for not immediately endorsing him, Pollard's strong defense is a refreshing change.

Note that Trump has secured the nomination prior to the June 7 Super Tuesday primary contests in the final five states. About 303 delegates will be up for grabs on that primary night.

Trump's nomination caps an incredible primary run where he competed against 16 other GOP contenders.

Recall that in the early stages of this weird and wacky primary season, Trump publicly called illegal Mexican immigrants "rapists." He promised to build a wall to keep out illegal Mexican immigrants. Also he called for banning Muslim immigrants to the United States until the government figured out how to protect its citizens and the country from radical Islamic terrorists infiltrating the country.

Yes, these comments were incendiary. And totally politically incorrect. But Trump, a master showman and entertainer, was able to effectively separate himself from the herd of much more politically experienced opponents.

Trump then brilliantly skewered his major opponents by giving them nasty but very appropriate sobriquets - "Lyin Ted" Cruz, "Little Marco" Rubio, and "Weak" Jeb Bush. These devastating nicknames stuck and helped define these very flawed candidates. None of them were able to survive.

Now Trump - with the GOP establishment slowly unifying behind him due to their shared hostility towards the presumptive Democratic nominee - has turned his exceptional personal PR guns against "Crooked" Hillary and "Slick Willie" Clinton.

The Clintons have never collectively faced such nasty and over the top public abuse and derision.

Hillary's campaign is already toast.

It is now just a question of how badly Trump will defeat Hillary in November.

June 8, 2016

Has The World Gone Trumpian? - Sexy Italian Film Stars Donald-Like Hero

★ ★ ★ ★ ★ ★ ★ ★ ★ ★ ★ ★ ★

(a film review)

*(**NOTE:** It is early June, 2016. Trump has secured a majority of the GOP delegates in the primaries. Hillary Clinton is still battling Sanders to secure her majority of the Democratic delegates and clinch her nomination.*

Once again, I have to escape from this political/primary bubble to test the cultural winds. On a whim I drop into a sexy European film, penned by an American writer. Strangely, one of the lead male characters strongly reminds me of The Donald. And it is no coincidence that this very erotic film is set on an Italian island where boatloads of illegal migrants from the Middle East are trying to land. And the threat of illegal immigrants is ever present.

Gorgeous babes, a Trump-like character and the threat of illegal immigrants. This American presidential election has permeated the international cultural environment. Trumpism has gone global. Leaping from America and now landing in European culture.)

Italian director Luca Guadagnino has taken the original 1969 French psychological thriller *La Piscine (The Swimming Pool)* and has, quite literally, fleshed out the main characters.

The film stars Tilda Swinton in the lead and Matthias Shoenaerts as her hot, younger lover, with Ralph Fiennes as Swinton's former lover and Dakota Johnson as the film's sexual ingénue. They spend most of the film naked or semi-naked, in and around the villa's sumptuous pool - swimming, sunning, fighting, and shagging.

Guided by a sexually charged screenplay penned by American writer David Kajganich, Guadagnino has helped Swinton and Fiennes craft some of their best, most memorable and, in my opinion, most Oscar-worthy performances in years.

Swinton (Academy Award winner for Best Supporting Actress in *Michael Clayton*) is superb as Marianne, a David Bowie-like female rock star who is recuperating from throat surgery and chilling out in a gorgeous, sprawling villa in the island's hills. Along with her is her bearded and brooding lover, Paul (Belgian actor Matthias Shoenaerts.)

Under doctor's orders, Marianne has been forbidden to use her voice, so she must wordlessly express her feelings throughout the film: Love, anger, fear, doubt, confusion, jealousy, betrayal, contentment, and orgiastic ecstasy. To do so, Swinton draws upon all her formidable acting skills. It is truly a tour de force of artistic achievement.

In the past, Swinton has typically played weird, asexual androgynous roles. As rock star Marianne - who George (Fiennes) describes as someone who loves to "fuck, fuck, and fuck" - she is very sexual and sensuous. In one of the opening scenes, she and her lover Paul are naked in the pool. Swinton's back is against the wall, and Paul thrusts inside her with her fully exposed and wonderful breasts all ablaze. A great scene that perfectly sets the stage for the wild ride to follow.

Fiennes, normally known for his powerful and dramatic roles in *The English Patient, Schindler's List,* and *The Constant Gardener,* lets it all hang out as the bearded, bombastic, and brash George Hawes. A wild and crazy music producer, George is a control freak with a devilish, snake-like smile. He is hedonistic, egotistical, sexist, selfish, narcissistic, abrasive, and, for most of the film, annoyingly obnoxious.

But he is very hard to look away from. He is, simply, captivating. George's over-the-top, cock-walking, Jagger-like dance at poolside to The Stones' "Emotional Rescue," is one of the true highlights of this film.

In other words, Fiennes as George is channeling the headline-grabbing Trumpster. I am not sure that this portrayal is by design or just mere coincidence.

Talk about art imitating life.

Seen through flashbacks, the viewer learns that, years ago, George helped produce Marianne's music. They were also coke-snorting lovers. As George ruefully admits, he lost Marianne back then because he cheated on her. He was always "slutting around." As a last attempt at controlling Marianne's life and fate, George introduced his then-young documentary filmmaker friend, Paul, to Marianne.

Now fast forward back to the present. George invades Marianne and Paul's idyllic and monogamous hideaway, nymphet daughter Penelope (Fanning) in tow. George has an agenda, and so does the sly Penelope. Both George and Penelope will force Marianne and Paul to deal with their respective addictions.

Ugly truths are revealed. Chests are bared. This story will not end well.

Interestingly, this story is set among the more serious and contemporary one of foreign migrants escaping the Middle East and trying desperately to reach Italy's shores. And dying in the process.

As George tries to rekindle Marianne's love for him during a shopping trip, the television in the background reveals that several migrants have drowned off the shore of the island where Marianne's villa sits. Those who survived the voyage from nearby Tunisia have been penned in detention centres on the island. Some immigrants have escaped and may be a threat to the locals.

Was the screenwriter and director trying to make a more important point?

That the lives and loves of these languorous four do not amount to a Sicilian hill of beans in the greater scheme, or "Bigger Splash," of things?

Or did the film director simply intend to take the original *La Piscine* and go deeper, bigger, and bawdier?

Or more probably, the screenwriter and director were also making the subtle point that, even in this idyllic setting, there are outside forces - i.e, hordes of illegal immigrants, who may adversely change this way of life forever. And probably not for the better.

June 11, 2016

Horrific Orlando Massacre About Radical Islamic Terrorism - Not About Trump

According to reliable reports an American citizen born to Afghan parents named Omar Mateen walked into an Orlando gay club, shot and killed 49 persons in the club and wounded dozens of others.

Reliable sources suggest that, prior to Mr. Mateen entering the club, he had phoned 911 and swore allegiance to ISIS. Further reports indicate that he was a "person of interest" to the FBI for over two years.

On the basis of these various reports, this was clearly a radical Islamic domestic terrorist act with the intent of killing gay American women and men.

Typically, the liberal-biased press is criticizing Trump for his tweets in response to this horrific event, as if blaming Trump for what had happened.

It appears that Democratic supporters and the liberal-biased press are either intentionally or unintentionally trying to divert attention from the real harsh reality, that this terrorist act was a failure of the Obama Administration to protect Americans.

This was also not a fault of lack of gun controls because Mr. Mateen, according to reliable reports, had a valid permit to carry a firearm.

In the coming days, we shall hear from the Obama Administration and from Hillary Clinton that this mass killing has nothing to do with Islam or the Muslim culture. That this was the act of a deranged, mentally ill lone wolf. And that the United States should be most concerned about painting all Muslims with the same racist, Islamophobic brush.

Also, Obama and Clinton will pompously claim that Trump is a horrible man and totally unsuitable to be president, because he is not acting "presidential" - because Trump is exposing what is patently clear to the majority of Americans.

That there are American citizens or landed immigrants or illegal immigrants in the United States who do not share such American values as equality between men and women. (There are reports that Mr. Mateen mistreated his former wife and beat her - surprise, surprise.)

These same radical Islamic persons and groups also do not share the same American values that respect sexual equality.

Unlike these cultures, Americans respect members of the LGBTQ community. And unlike radical Islamic culture, in America these people are not considered filth or lowlifes who deserve to be gunned down like animals.

It is about time that the Obamas, the Clintons, the liberal press of the *Washington Post, New York Times*, CNN and MSNBC get their clueless heads out of the sand, put their political correctness in abeyance, and face the harsh reality that there are serious and dangerous radical Islamic men and women in the U.S. who want to kill and maim Americans because these Americans do not share, or refuse to adopt, the highly dangerous values, beliefs and culture of radical Islam.

June 13, 2016

Did Liberal Democratic Political Correctness Play a Role in Orlando Shooting?

✶ ✶ ✶ ✶ ✶ ✶ ✶ ✶ ✶ ✶ ✶ ✶ ✶

Recently I posted a comment on the horrific Orlando shooting by a known American radical Islamist. In doing so I commented that at first the American liberal-biased press went after Trump for his politically incorrect comments in the wake of the murder and mayhem. As if to distract the American people from the real cause of this mass murder of gay people and people who were in attendance at an Orlando gay bar.

I predicted that Obama and Hillary's responses would be to ignore that a known radical Islamist had killed these unfortunate people. And that instead these clueless and irresponsible liberal leaders, out of political correctness, would stress the need for gun control and caution tolerance against Islamophobia.

Predictably the response from my liberal friends was to employ Obama's favorite rhetorical "straw dog" argument: Argue against a position that has not been advanced by his critics. In other words, respond to this horrible killing by playing the "Jewish immigrant" card:

"Oh woe is me. If you are against radical Islamists who kill innocent gay men and women, then you and your racist kind must be against Jewish people in the 1930s fleeing Nazi Germany?"

Or: "Mitch, is Trump's solution to deport all Muslims from America?"

Or: "Mitch, are you in favor of incarcerating all Muslim Canadians as was done to Japanese-Canadians in Canada during World War II?"

How about, for a modest start, we try coming to some agreement or consensus as to the problem?

The problem for Canadian liberals (Liberals, NDP, progressives) and American liberals (Democrats) is they believe that there is a moral equivalence between their own immigrant experience and the experience of radical Islamic immigrants who live and work in Canada and the U.S. (Whether they be citizens, landed immigrants or illegal immigrants or refugees from the Middle East).

In other words to these politically correct and misguided liberals, all cultures are alike and the values and beliefs of radical Islamics should be respected equally.

But radical Islamists are different from the waves and waves of immigrant groups who have come to North

America in the last 150 years - the Irish, the Jews, Italians, Greeks, Asians, South Asians, Latin Americans, Eastern Europeans, Russians, just to name a few. For the most part, members of these immigrant groups came to North America looking for a better life for themselves and their children and though retaining their cultures to a degree, for the most part they assimilated into the greater North American culture.

These various cultures adopted over time the predominant North American value which values women equally to men, (i.e. gender equality) and respects sexual equality (the LGBT community.)

When was the last time that an Irish, Jewish, Italian, South Asian, Asian fellow in the last 150 years walked into a Florida gay bar, blew away 49 people and injured another 53 people because he did not like the fact that these victims adopted a gay lifestyle?

When was the last time in 150 years that a group of Jewish, Italian, South Asian, Asian, Eastern European men surrounded, raped, sexually assaulted, abused and assaulted over 1,000 women in the city of Cologne, Germany? No one is suggesting to you" head in the sand" liberals that all Muslims should be deported from North America.

That is the typical Obamian "straw man" rhetorical response, where Obama tries to refute an argument never advanced by his critics. How about first calling a spade a spade? That the killer who blew away all these helpless victims in Orlando was a radical Islamic terrorist. That the men who raped and sexually assaulted over 1000 women in Cologne were Islamists who treat women as garbage and chattels.

The largest mass shooting in US history was preventable. Lack of gun control did not kill these victims. But liberal political correctness prevented American law enforcement officials from doing their job, and the liberals' myopia to the dangers of radical Islamists should also take some responsibility.

June 13, 2016

Orlando Massacre Occurred on Obama's Watch. Where's the Outrage against Obama?

* * * * * * * * * * * * *

Words do matter.

Ever since it was publicly disclosed that the killer of 49 persons in the Orlando gay club was a known Muslim extremist who had been under FBI surveillance, President Barack Obama has failed to properly identify the murderer as a radical Islamic terrorist.

Obama's refusal to so identify is indicative of Obama and his administration's failure to acknowledge that there is a serious threat of domestic radical Islamic terrorism within the borders of the United States.

Obama's negligence in this regard has trickled down to his Justice Department and to federal law enforcement agencies in the U.S.

The FBI has described Omar Mateen, the man who shot and killed forty-nine persons and injured over fifty other patrons of the Orlando gay club, as a "person of interest."

He had been twice picked up by the FBI in the last two years, interviewed and investigated, then let go.

Unofficial sources within and without the FBI allege that Omar Mateen was let go by the FBI and not arrested or put on surveillance due to the political correctness of the Obama Administration. Obama and his close advisers in his Administration have made it patently clear to all Justice officials from the top on down that unduly arresting or putting on surveillance men of Islamic faith was akin to racial profiling and contrary to such American rights as freedom of religion and freedom of expression. And contrary to the fundamental tenets of America as a free and tolerant multicultural society.

Those are all fine and noble sentiments in principle. But the fact is Obama's overwhelming opposition to publicly identifying radical Islamic terrorism has had the effect of handcuffing the work of the FBI and all federal security agencies in their role as protecting Americans from terrorism.

The Orlando massacre was certainly preventable but for Obama's head in the sand and very soft approach to domestic radical Islamic terrorism.

It is interesting to note that, notwithstanding that Omar Mateen had called 911 and pledged his support for ISIS prior to the Orlando massacre, Obama's first public response was a pathetic misrepresentation that this was merely a hate crime.

Note that Hillary Clinton, who has tied her faltering presidential campaign to Obama's failed presidency, weakly echoed Obama's approach to the worst mass killing in US history.

It was only several hours later - and I am sure after extensive focus grouping - that the spineless Obama grudgingly admitted that a terrorist act had been committed.

Obama's puppet Hillary then changed her public position and came out echoing her former boss that in fact a terrorist act had been committed.

To date Obama has failed to recognize that this was in fact a radical Islamic terrorist act for fear of alienating his leftist "head in the sand" liberals who cannot bring themselves to believe that radical Islamists hate gays and believe they should be killed and eradicated from a preferred Sharia-based society.

In public remarks on Tuesday Obama further used the specious argument that identifying the killer as a radical Muslim would further inflame Muslims and ISIS to commit further atrocities against Americans.

Clearly by these comments Obama is more concerned about not hurting the feelings of American Muslims and not inflaming further the anti-American/anti-western feelings of ISIS - a brutal and murderous bunch of Muslim terrorists and thugs - than the feelings of fellow non Muslim Americans who are being terrorized by these people.

Further, Obama had the chutzpah to instead focus on weak gun control as the raison d'etre for this horrific massacre - not the culture of radical Islam which hates gays and the gay lifestyle.

Lastly Obama had the gall to blame the American people for being intolerant towards the gay lifestyle. As if the American people pulled the trigger and wiped out forty-nine lives.

Clearly Obama has stayed too long at the party. The sooner he leaves the political scene the better.

And since Hillary has tied her failing campaign to a leader who will forever be remembered as being soft on domestic Islamic terrorism and for failing to protect American lives, Hillary Clinton's hopes of being the first female American president died in that Orlando gay club too.

June 15, 2016

Sluggish Barack Hussein "Muhammad Ali" Obama II Knocked Out by the More Formidable Counter Puncher Donald "Joe Frazier" Trump

* * * * * * * * * * * * *

Obama, who is usually too cool to school his opponents, tried to channel his inner Muhammad (Ali) a few days ago.

As he has done in the past - float like a butterfly and verbally sting like a freaking bee, with his blinding fast one-two rhetorical fisticuffs.

Except on this occasion time had clearly taken its toll on this graying and sluggish Chicago community street organizer-turned-president. Obama is in his eighth and last year of his presidency. And it showed. He was no longer the young and nimble verbal pugilist, easily beating up the slow moving John McCain or the solid but unoriginal Romney.

The once great black (and white) hope (and change) candidate was a mere shadow of his former self. Felled by over-exposure all these years in front of the cameras.

Weakened by his own overblown rhetoric. Undermined by America's growing recognition, that behind his rhetorical flourishes, he was just an empty Canali suit.

Clearly no longer nimble. With just feet of clay.

Ironically, over the years the more Obama held forth from his presidential bully pulpit - trying to lead, inspire and persuade - the more he weakened and undermined himself.

Until he had become a mere caricature of himself.

Blah, Blah, Blah, Blah

Obama had reduced himself to mere sound and fury, signifying nothing.

This time Obama was facing a formidable New York street fighter: Trump, the Queens Bomber. Who did not play by prescribed Washington political rules.

Trump made up his own rules and then he played fast and loose with them.

In the wake of the horrific Orlando shooting where 49 persons had been killed and over 53 people had been injured, Trump did not call for national unity, as in the wake of 9/11.

Instead Trump unleashed a withering attack on Obama immediately after the Orlando massacre, the worst mass terrorist shooting in American history, which occurred as Trump had predicted on Obama's watch.

Instead Trump publicly accused Obama of being weak, indecisive and incompetent. And much, much worse.

Trump boldly suggested that the murderer, Omar Mateen, a radical Islamic terrorist, was well known to the FBI but had been permitted to roam freely into the Orlando gay club and kill at will due to Obama's political correctness. In other words, thanks to Obama and his administration's failure to come down hard on suspected radical Islamic terrorists.

Unlike previous opponents Trump attacked Obama where Obama was most vulnerable.

Trump may have some obvious faults but he has brilliant political instincts, and an uncanny ability to intuit his opponents' fatal weaknesses: "Lying Ted" Cruz, "weak Jeb" Bush, "cowardly" Mittens Romney.

In Obama's case Trump zeroed in on Obama's failure throughout his entire presidency to properly identify any murderous Muslims as radical Islamic terrorists.

It was publicly disclosed and verified that the killer was a Muslim who had been influenced to commit a horrific terrorist act because of his religious Islamic beliefs in the service of ISIS. Obama, predictably as he had done in the wake of previous radical Islamic terrorist acts on American soil (Fort Hood and San Bernardino), just could not bring himself to identify the killer as a radical Islamic terrorist.

Obama first called the act a mere hate crime.

Then he called it a terrorist act.

Then Obama tried to dismiss the known Islamic killer as a mentally deranged lone wolf.

Then he tried to rationalize his failure to call a spade a spade. According to Obama the killer was just an extremist who had perverted Islam for his own evil purposes.

To Obama and his many clueless and delusional supporters this horrible mass murder of mostly gay men and women had nothing to do with Islam but was carried out by an extremist who was not really Muslim.

Say what?

Then of course predictably, Obama went on the offensive and attacked Trump for being a racist, an Islamophobe.

For unfairly tarnishing the whole peaceful religion of Islam. For casting aspersions on all Muslim Americans.

For fomenting intolerance and hatred against Muslims and aiding and abetting the enemy – ISIS - by inciting more Muslims to attack America due to Trump's own rhetoric.

Obama further attacked Trump for being against freedom of religion. For proposing that immigrant Muslims be temporarily banned from entering the United States which according to Obama was against American values.

Obama aided and abetted by his liberal press lackeys expected Trump to fold like a cheap suit.

But Trump did not collapse under Obama's withering public attack.

Instead Trump fought back harder, tougher and deadlier.

Trump counter punched that Obama had come across more sympathetic to the radical Islamic terrorist and his Islamic supporters who supported these mass killings than the actual victims of this horrific act.

Trump further hammered Obama by arguing that Obama was more upset with Trump's attacks than the actual attack of this murderous radical Islamic terrorist thug who killed and injured over one hundred gay men and women.

And that is the key!

Obama's reluctance to identify this killer as a radical Islamic terrorist is because, in Obama's head and his heart, this Muslim and all Muslims like this Omar Mateen are the real victims of American and European imperialism.

In Obama's head (channeling and heavily influenced by his leftist anti-imperialistic Kenyan Muslim father, Barack Hussein Obama Sr.) Islam is a peaceful religion and all these terrorist acts by ISIS, ISIL, the Taliban and al Qaeda are done by extremists who are not real Muslims.

That is why Obama can't bring himself to call these terrorists by their right name as radical Islamic terrorists.

That is why Obama has handcuffed American federal and police authorities from properly doing their jobs and arresting all these known Islamic potential terrorists.

That is why Obama (and his power-hungry lackey Hillary Clinton) has no problem opening up the floodgates to Muslims from all the Mideast countries to invade America as they have done in Europe.

That is why Obama and his puppet Clinton are unable and incapable of protecting Americans from further radical Islamic terrorist attacks.

Because, to Obama, Muslims are always the victims. Americans are always the perpetrators. And these jihadist acts are the will of Allah.

This past week Trump knocked down Obama for the count and dealt a fatal blow to the presidency of this American-born but anti-American Kenyan.

June 17, 2016

Is Trump More a Friend to Gays and Women than Hillary?

In Trump's first major rally after the Orlando nightclub massacre by a home-grown American radical Islamic terrorist, Trump lashed out at Hillary for sacrificing the rights of the LGBT community and women on the altar of political correctness.

In other words, Hillary has chosen to support the rights of Mideast Muslim immigrants and refugees (many of whom are sympathetic to radical Islam - which is hostile to gay people and treat women as chattels deserving of sexual abuse) over the rights of members of America's growing LGBT communities and the rights and freedoms from abuse of American women.

There is a clear and undeniable connection between Islam's hatred of gays (for perverting Islam and all its adherents - see numerous passages in the Koran) and the murderous actions of radical Muslim terrorist Omar Mateen, who intentionally killed and wounded mostly gay men and women at an Orlando club.

Since 9/11 and certainly for the last eight years of the Obama Administration, Hillary has failed to make that connection. She has often called Islam a religion of peace and members of al Qaeda, ISIS and the Taliban as "extremists" who are not real Muslims, but have perverted the noble and peaceful teachings of Islam for their own evil purposes.

Hillary, together with many Democrats and members of the left, are deluding themselves as to the very real threat of radical Islamists to the lives and liberties of American gay people and American women.

So Hillary can have her ideological cake and eat it too.

Hillary and most Democrats and members of the left are caught in the narrative that Muslims are the victims of American and European imperialism, white supremacy, racism and colonialism. And as such, America should open up its borders to these poor immigrants and refugees out of liberal guilt.

According to Hillary and the left, the murderous followers of ISIS, al Qaeda and the Taliban are not really Muslims, since Islam is a peaceful religion. Instead Hillary, along with Obama, treats these terrorists as people who have been adversely influenced by some extreme unnamed ideology.

What - Judaism, Buddhism and Hinduism?

The teachings of Yoga?

But the real and practical consequences of this delusion and denial are the horrible deaths of gay Americans in Orlando, innocent Americans in San Bernardino, and innocent American soldiers in Fort Hood - all due to radical Islamic terrorism which Obama and Hillary refuse to name, identify and acknowledge.

Trump has brilliantly exploded the myth of the peaceful Muslim.

And he has brilliantly undermined Hillary's claim that she and she alone can stand up for the rights of America's gay community and American women.

Because face it, radical Muslims kill gays. They shoot them to death. They drop them from buildings. They stone them and torture them. These same radical Muslims enslave women. They sexually abuse them and treat them like cattle.

By her actions and public declarations, Hillary has clearly chosen radical Muslims at the expense of American gays and American women.

There is no question in my mind that Trump will pick up support from these two very important groups, because many members of these groups will choose their life and personal security over political correctness.

June 17, 2016

Social Media Erupts over Trump, Islam as Peaceful Religion and Democratic pro Black Lives Matter/Muslim/Leftist anti-Semitism and anti-Israel

* * * * * * * * * * * * *

(NOTE: I have many friends who are conservatives and are staunchly anti-Trump. Of course there are those conservatives on the fence and others are extremely pro Trump. I also have many friends who live and work on the dark side - that is, as card-carding leftists and liberals and the odd socialist thrown in for the sake of diversity. Fortunately they read my stuff and critically comment with passion and commitment. Though they are mostly wrong-headed, sometimes they are right [or left as the case may be.] The very energetic discussion that follows reflects that diversity of interest.)

Liberal Friend (name withheld by request): Uh, no! To your credit Mitch, you have maintained a progressive point of view on many social issues – women's rights and marriage equality as examples. However, Trump agrees with the right-wing social conservatives, who have social views much more similar to the Islamic extremists you and I correctly condemn.

Jeff: "Trump has brilliantly exploded the myth of the peaceful Muslim?" Yes only Trump did that. Hilarious. You've lost it, Mitch.

And by adopting Trump's racist claims that there are no peaceful Muslims as you put it, you adopt and own his racism. Shameful.

Paul: When did Islamic terrorist become a race?

Jeff: Brilliant retort. Call him a racist, bigot, xenophobe. Doesn't matter, he's all of those and I think you know what I mean.

Paul: Jeff, I know that those who oppose Trump have grown violent and extreme. I know hyperbole when I hear or read it. I know that sanity left the building a long time ago with respect to dogmatic progressives.

Jeff: I'm as conservative as they get. A real conservative not like Trump. Mitch says Trump brilliantly exposed the myth of the peaceful Muslim. Not a single peaceful Muslim in the world. That's not hyperbole? This is the very definition of bigotry Paul so you can own it too.

Paul: Jeff, I'll challenge you on the only significant point of fact in your remark. Please direct me to a credible report where Trump states that there is "Not a single peaceful

Muslim in the world". I certainly would not support a statement like that.

Jeff: Paul, that was Mitch's take. What would you say the myth of the peaceful Muslim means?

Paul: Jeff, I view it as a reaction to the predictable reaction of politicians to remind us to not blame Islam after every Islamic terrorist attack since 9/11. It's become pat.

After 9/11 there was a very legitimate fear that outrage would bleed into insanity and innocent people who appeared to the uninformed to be of Middle Eastern heritage would be beaten or gunned down in the streets. I lived next door to an elderly Italian couple and a Pakistani family who wore cultural garb. We made it a point to hang out with them in their yard in solidarity because they were afraid for their safety. Fortunately, we are better than that and the world did not erupt in violence against Muslims. This was not the result of liberal pandering but of our humanity. A humanity that is lacking in radical Islamics.

These politicians are no longer acting in the public interest by using the veil of promoting a claim that is not at risk by ignoring the threat of Islamic violence. The "Religion of Peace" platitude is a cop-out.

Jeff: I absolutely agree and well said. Check dozens of posts on my time line if you like. There were at least a half-dozen serious, qualified Republican candidates who would also agree with that. Nothing justifies the fraud Trump who immediately wantonly politicized the Orlando attack without a hint of condolence.

Paul: We've found common ground for sure. I consider Trump a megalomaniac blowhard who may identify systemic problems (which would be good) but lacks the grace and intellect to effect positive change.

Hillary is so tainted by her lies, scandals and obvious role as establishment puppet that she is beyond consideration. If they can't have a do-over, I'll take Trump but I won't be buying any bumper stickers.

Mitch: Gentlemen, I commend you all for your very thoughtful, reasoned and provocative statements. I am honored that you have participated with such passion on this timeline. Interestingly, with the exception of my good friend Liberal Friend, and my Harvard classmate, good friend and former Harvard Crimson editor, you all share conservative views. So it is fascinating to me to read and see the debate that is playing out in the conservative camp over Trump's candidacy.

Liberal Friend, let me try to address your point about Trump attracting the support of staunch social conservatives who hold views to which I do not subscribe. Yes, I pride myself on being to the left on most social issues. I am staunchly pro-choice, same sex marriage, pro-LGBTQ. I am a third generation ethnic minority Jew, whose great grandparents, the Salomon clan, and grandparents, the Wolfe clan, were immigrants to Canada. My family has been voting Liberal in Canada since the 1880s. So I come by these views naturally.

The political genius of Trump is that unlike Reagan, the Bushes I and II, McCain and Romney, Trump won the GOP primaries without unduly pandering to the social conservative wing of the party, i.e. the Christian evangelicals.

This thrice married New York/Queens dude from blue state New York, who is the very embodiment of "New York values", according to Lying Ted Cruz, (pro-gay, pro-sex, pro-Planned Parenthood, pro-divorce, pro-gambling, pro-women, pro-racial and ethnic minorities and all kinds of other sins, LOL) killed Cruz in the Christian evangelical heartlands by doing something that all his predecessors failed to do: Dealing with these people's bread and butter economic issues. Their loss of jobs, their underemployment, unemployment, their loss of dignity, losing their homes in the face of an economy (bad free trade deals, bank bailouts) that appears to be fixed to the benefit of the economic elites in Wall Street, and on the west coast.

These working class GOP and Dems realized that they had been used by the GOP Washington political elites, and the 1% Romneys and Bushes, who threw these GOP supporters social conservative scraps (anti-abortion, anti-same sex marriage stuff) in order to secure their support so they, the political elites, could reduce taxes, social security, the safety net, all to their own economic and financial benefit.

Yes, Liberal Friend, Trump has supporters whose socially conservative views do not jibe with mine, but his mandate has been based on his economic policies, i.e. better free trade deals, bringing manufacturing jobs back to the US, being tougher on America's trading partners like China, Japan and Europe. And forcing the latter, Japan and Europe, to share the costs of their defense.

As to your remarks, Harvard Friend, of course I am concerned with anti-Semitism in the GOP party. But I am pleased that Trump has come out 100% in favor of Israel and like his fellow New Yorker, Dem New York Senator Chuck Schumer - the older brother of our brilliant classmate Fran Schumer - he believes that the Iranian deal was a horrible deal for the US and even worse, for one of the US key allies, Israel.

Note Hillary was leaning against the Iranian deal before she was in favor of it. Hillary only cares about Hillary and what will grease her way to the presidency.

I also recall you, Harvard Friend, have written how Hillary and Bill Clinton screwed the Haitian people, backing its corrupt president and probably benefitting financially in the process. Also wasn't it your very own journal, the incomparable Nation, that published a devastating anti-Hillary piece, by a black female writer lambasting Hillary and Bill for screwing thousands of American blacks in the 1990s, with Clinton's anti-black welfare reform policies and pro law and order policies which unfairly imprisoned thousands of black men and destroyed thousands of black families and destroyed many black communities. But I digress.

Ironically, the Christian evangelicals who form an important element of the GOP party are staunchly pro Israel and pro Israeli democracy. As a result, for the most part, the GOP before Trump and now under Trump, are very pro Israel and as such pro Jewish.

What is fascinating to me and very disturbing - and should be very disturbing to you, Harvard Friend - is how horribly anti-Israeli and anti-Semitic the Democratic Party has become, and the left who form the backbone of the Democratic party.

Though I am pro Zionist, I appreciate that some of Israeli's domestic and foreign policies should be subject to legitimate criticism and opposition. I can't think of any at the moment (LOL) but I am sure there are one or two.

However, under the guise and shelter of legitimate criticism, the Hamas-inspired anti-Israeli and pro anti-Semitic BDS movement has arisen on many liberal-oriented, pro Democratic universities. This anti-Semitic BDS movement has now merged with the anti-Semitic leftist narrative that all Arabs, Palestinians, and Muslims are victims of Israeli/American imperialism and aggression. In the Democratic Party you now have a toxic stew of cancerous Black Lives Matter/Muslim/ leftist anti-Semitism, that unfortunately has thrived and metastasized during Obama's politically correct, pro diversity, racially-tinged, anti-Israel presidency.

Harvard Friend, three years ago, I wrote a piece for the American *Huffington Post* entitled, "Where is the Feminist Outrage over Discrimination in Gaza?"

This piece sadly still resonates today. Where is the outrage by the left and the Democrats over Arab/Muslim discrimination against gays and women? We are not talking about unequal wages! We are talking about many homophobic Muslim countries where homosexuality is punished with death, stoning, throwing off of buildings, torture. The same holds true for the treatment of women in these countries. Unfortunately, these values are shared by many American Muslims and their children. Where is the outrage of the left and of the Democrats to American Muslims who believe that their religion gives them the right to kill, punish and mistreat gays? Or gives them the right to rape, sexually abuse, assault and abuse women?

Where is the outrage of the left to these un-American values? Where is the outrage in the left and in the Democratic Party to singling out and vilifying Israel for all the ills of the Palestinians, the Arabs in the Mideast? Where is the outrage of the left and of the Democratic Party and of your President for Palestinians knifing to death innocent Israelis?

Whether Trump wins or loses, to his credit he has exposed the cancerous anti-Semitic, anti-gay, anti-female underbelly of the left and of the Democratic Party.

June 20, 2016

Who Do You Believe- Biased Liberal Polls or Your Gut Political Instincts?

The recent poll taken by Reuters/Ipsos in mid June, around the time of the horrible Orlando shooting, has Hillary Clinton enjoying a solid eleven-point lead over Donald Trump.

According to such heavily biased liberal pundits and Trump haters as Frank Bruni of the *New York Times* and Michael Tomasky of the *Daily Beast,* Donald Trump is dead in the water.

I can just see the men and women in the Trump-hating newsrooms of the *Washington Post*, *Politico*, CNN and the *New York Times* high-fiving and doing happy dances around their fair trade espresso machines.

The nervous nellies in the Republican Party, the Bushes and Romneys, still smarting and seething from Trump's defeat of their dreams and humiliation of their favored candidates are also secretly rejoicing, and reviving their ridiculous plans to defeat Trump in the July GOP convention.

It is truly a sad commentary on the ignorance and shallowness of these so-called political experts and career politicians that they have substituted political smarts, savvy and intelligence with inaccurate polls skewered to obtain their desired results by biased polling techniques.

Polling a couple of thousand voters, where more Democrats are polled than GOP, does not make for an accurate projection of ultimate electoral success.

Furthermore, a majority of the eligible voters Reuters/Ipsos polled were surveyed prior to the Orlando mass murder by Omar Mateen of 49 gay men and women. An event which was certainly a political game changer.

Furthermore, when Trump secured the GOP nomination, there was a bump in his numbers to the same level of support for Hillary.

It was predictable that once Hillary secured the Democratic nomination, there would be a temporary bump in Hillary's numbers.

But it appears because of Hillary's continued support for Islam, whose religion and culture promote the punishment and killing of gay people and the abuse, torture and enslavement of women, and her failure to acknowledge that Islamists persecute gays and women, Hillary's honeymoon will be short-lived.

It is more noteworthy that since Orlando, a majority of Americans support Trump's temporary ban on Muslims immigrating to the United States.

Pivoting even more to the centre in an effort to reach out to disaffected independents and Democrats, Trump refined his message by proposing that his temporary ban would be limited to immigrants from known terrorist countries that posed a threat to America and its European allies.

In his speech, Trump specifically stated:

> *"When I'm elected, I will suspend immigration from areas of the world where there's a proven history of terrorism against the United States, Europe or our allies until we fully understand how to end these threats," he said. "After a full … long overdue security assessment we will develop a responsible immigration policy that serves the interests and values of America."*

Trump explicitly criticized Hillary Clinton, for failing to recognize the reality of the threat that confronts America and the western world:

> *Just a few weeks before San Bernardino, the slaughter, that's all it was was a slaughter, Hillary Clinton explained her refusal to say the words "radical Islam." Here is what she said, exact quote: "Muslims are peaceful and tolerant people, and have nothing whatsoever to do with terrorism." That is Hillary Clinton. …*
>
> *We cannot continue to allow thousands upon thousands of people to pour into our country many of whom have the same thought process as this savage killer. Many of the principles of radical Islam are incompatible with Western values and institutions.*

> *Remember this, radical Islam is anti-woman, anti-gay and anti-American.*
>
> *I refuse to allow America to become a place where gay people, Christian people, Jewish people are targets of persecution and intimidation by radical Islamic preachers of hate and violence.*
>
> *This is not just a national security issue. It's a quality of life issue. If we want to protect the quality of life for all Americans - women and children, gay and straight, Jews and Christians and all people then we need to tell the truth about radical Islam and we need to do it now.*

Though this is not being reported in the mainstream liberal press, my associates and I who cover many American gay-oriented Facebook sites have been noticing more positive comments about Trump within the LGBT American community. And more gay members coming out in favor of Trump for publicly standing up for the LGBT community against an Islamic religion and culture that at its fundamentalist core persecutes, prosecutes, punishes and kills gay people.

Accordingly, the current polls are stale-dated and wrong.

Trump is in reality leading Hillary by 5 points and he is pulling away from her.

June 20, 2016

Social Media Debates Pro-Hillary Polls and Assesses Her Real Chances

★ ★ ★ ★ ★ ★ ★ ★ ★ ★ ★ ★ ★

(NOTE: My piece generated some vigorous reactions on Facebook from liberal anti-Trump types and from conservative anti-Trump pundits as well. Here is a sampling of this very interesting and vigorous debate, in which I, of course, had to pontificate and argue as well.)

Jeff: One consistent thing about the Trump non-campaign from the start is how they love every poll that has ever had him out front. Consistently, every poll that had him behind Hillary which is by far the majority, are liberal hit job sleazy pollsters. As I've said before Mitch and despite the Republican primaries, if no women, Hispanics, blacks, other minorities, College educated whites show up to vote in November I think Trumpie stands a really good chance.

Mitch: Well, Jeff, my man, you have been consistent. But you must agree that Trump is right in calling out radical Muslims whose religion and culture promote the persecution of gays and women. While Obama and Hillary can't bring themselves to utter the words radical Islamic terrorist, let alone admit that just about all Muslim countries persecute, prosecute and oftentimes kill gays.

Mark: It's really interesting to me. I'm old enough (barely) to remember almost the exact same treatment of Ronald Reagan in 1980. They had Carter being re-elected all through the campaign. Then, near the end of the campaign, the polls sputtered but all the "experts" said Carter would eke out a narrow re-election victory. The night of the election all the bobble heads intoned "it would be a long night" to decide such a close, tight election. Of course it was over about 20 minutes after the polls closed and Ronald Reagan thumped Carter 50-41% and pulverized him 489-49 electoral votes, carrying 44 states. I think history will repeat itself in November of 2016.

Mitch: Mark, I am old enough to remember that like Obama and Hillary, Carter was a terribly weak leader especially in foreign affairs. In Carter's time, Iran took advantage of Carter's weakness and seized the American embassy in Tehran and took Americans there as hostages. Similarly, Iran has taken advantage of Obama's weakness, his desire for a legacy and his unAmerican-like sympathy for the Muslim cause in the Mideast and hence Obama caved to a terrible deal in favor of Iran. We now have learned that Iran lied, surprise, surprise- and was engaged in the development of a secret nuclear bomb in its secret military facility at Parchin. Iran has banned everyone including the US from inspecting this facility pursuant to Obama's sell out nuclear deal with the murderous Iran. As always Hillary was against the Iranian nuclear deal before she was in favor of it. I believe that Hillary will lose to Trump as Carter caved to Reagan.

Mark: I absolutely agree, Mitch. I hope we're both right. I'm losing friends by the dozen b/c I support Trump. But I don't care. I really think the country & the world is in for a shocker on election night. What do you make of this latest Trump scandal-de-jour about Lewandowski?

Mitch: Mark, firing Lewandowski was a brilliant move. Lew had done his job with the GOP primaries. But Trump needs to ramp up and broaden his appeal, which he will do with the much smarter political strategist Paul Manfort. Manfort will firm up GOP support behind Trump, build up the infrastructure, the ground game and broaden fund-raising and then go after the undecided, the independents, and the many millions who can't see crooked and corrupt Hillary as the president. Trump is nimble and quick. Hillary is the Titanic heading for the proverbial iceberg. Her organization is too large, too bureaucratic and reminds me of Jeb Bush who had the funds, but was humiliated by Trump's political agility and smarts and great instincts. Hillary is top heavy in management and her support is soft and shallow, unlike Obama in 2008. She is still a horrible campaigner. She looks like she would rather have root canal than give a speech to the faithful. She is toast.

June 22, 2016

Prediction: English Brexit Group To Crush Remain Group and Make Britain Great Britain Again!

* * * * * * * * * * * * *

Led by Boris Johnson, the charismatic former mayor of London, I predict that England will vote overwhelmingly to leave the overly bureaucratic and very unpopular European Union. Thus fatally destroying the political career of current Conservative Prime Minister David Cameron, who was a key supporter of the "Remain" faction.

Britons want their country back again. They want to make Great Britain Great again. They want control of their borders and control who should be allowed to immigrate to England.

These Britons rightfully fear that there is a special deal with Turkey to permit them to join the European Union in the future and allow millions of residents of Turkey (read: Radical Muslims) to settle in England outside the control of English political leaders.

Established English political leaders from both the left

and the right are shocked that the people are not following their advice.

Wow. Surprise, surprise.

Political correctness has blinded these pro-Muslim immigrant pols to the fact that a significant number of these immigrants are not integrating into British life. They have brought their Sharia anti-female, anti-gay culture to the English shores.

The Brexit supporters are not racist or anti-immigrant. They just want immigrants to integrate into English life and contribute to the vitality of English culture, and not try to undermine core English values of sexual equality and gender equality.

This is a referendum as to who is on the right side of history. The pro-British sovereignists/Euro skeptics/anti-Muslim immigrant Britons or the pro EU/pro-Islam-is-a-peaceful-religion/head-in-the-sand elitists.

The threats of doom and gloom by British pols and EU poobahs have fallen on deaf ears. Recall that Obama stupidly weighed in on this local debate and alienated many Britons with his typically tone deaf and arrogant support of the Remain forces.

The whole "Remain" effort has been a disaster and the Brexits will rule once the referendum votes are counted tomorrow.

June 27, 2016

Hillary Clinton - Hexit Stage Left

* * * * * * * * * * * * *

The overwhelming Brexit vote was a symbolic "screw you" by the British people to British political elites such as Conservative Prime Minister David Cameron and Labour leader Jeremy Corbyn. Because these very same political leaders had been contemptuous and insensitive to the very people who had elected them.

In addition to the British political establishment and the social/financial elites of London being the clear losers in this Brexit vote, other clear losers across the Atlantic were the equally arrogant and insensitive lame duck president Barack Hussein Obama II and his heir presumptive Hillary Clinton, who were staunch supporters of the status quo - the anti-populist Remain side.

Donald Trump, much criticized by the clueless and biased liberal American media, once again demonstrated his superior political instincts by clearly and vociferously coming out well in advance of the Brexit vote for the ultimately victorious Brexit side.

The success of Brexit demonstrates that Trump is on the right side of history and in the forefront of the significant populist changes that are sweeping the western free world, against liberal elitist political correctness. Against lib/elitist reckless disregard for Islamic jihadism. Against lib/elitist disregard to the threats of such core western values as the rule of English law (versus religious-based Sharia law,) gender equality and sexual equality.

On the other hand, this entire Brexit story has exposed once again that both Obama and Hillary are insensitive and arrogant Washington insider elites who are at their core - and as much as their transatlantic counterparts Cameron and Corbyn - contemptuous of the views and struggles of average working class people. They are also reckless in their disregard of the very real threat of Islamic jihadism infiltrating America.

Accordingly, both Obama and Hillary will meet the same fate of British PM Cameron who recently announced his resignation and his humiliating exit from political life.

In the case of Hillary Clinton: Hexit stage left.

In the case of lame duck Barack Hussein Obama the Second: "Who's your Daddy, now?"

June 28, 2016

The Brexit Revolt Caught Clinton with her Signature Pantsuit Down

★ ★ ★ ★ ★ ★ ★ ★ ★ ★ ★ ★ ★

I have said this and written this at least over a hundred times: Hillary Clinton has the worst political instincts and judgment.

Who else but Clinton would have as her key political slogan the horribly bland and politically tone deaf slogan "Stronger Together"? The same slogan as the British Remain faction which went down to humiliating defeat at the hands of over 17 million angry British voters - the Brexiteers, the common folk, living and working largely outside affluent and elitist downtown London.

The *New York Times* has reported that she and Slick Willy have worried for months that Hillary is out of sync with these turbulent and revolutionary times. Ya think?!

Hillary is not only out of sync, she is the very symbol of the arrogant, self-centred, power hungry, money grubbing American political establishment which puts its interests above the democratic masses. Which is indifferent, clueless and contemptuous of the strongly-held views, needs and wants of this basic, but very important American political bloc that cuts across all party, class, racial, ethnic, gender and socio-economic lines.

Damn right Hillary and Slick Willy should be scared. They should be really scared.

Because Hillary is not on the right side of history.

Hillary is the Titanic of left/liberal international establishment politics: Seemingly indestructible. Slow moving. Cautious. Oblivious to the huge populist iceberg up ahead. She barely perceives its tip. But below its surface this populist iceberg is growing a hundred times larger beneath the roiling political seas in which the Bad Ship Hillary chugs along. Her icy nemesis grows rapidly and daily. Quietly. Out of sight of her clueless myopic liberal politics. Out of sight, and therefore for the clueless arrogant Hillary, out of mind.

But this dangerous and destructive populist iceberg is waiting patiently for her. To destroy Hillary once and for all.

To sink all her political dreams that she has nurtured practically from birth.

Because the similarities between the successful Brexit achievement and this American presidential election are stark and bang-on.

Over seventeen million Brits who supported the winning Brexit voted among other things against the very brutal negative effects and collateral damage of globalized markets (i.e. the lack of job protection in free trade agreements, leading to the loss of traditional working class and middle income local jobs,) porous borders that permitted illegal immigrants to jump the line ahead of more worthy and legal immigrants. Against the very real and dangerous threat of immigrants and migrants entering their country with values that seriously undermined the core and essence of British sovereignty and identity - the English common law system (as opposed to religious-based Sharia law) and such core British values as true and unfettered freedom of speech and expression and respect for gender equality and sexual equality.

It is no coincidence that Hillary explicitly supported her hubby Bill's North American Free Trade Agreement, which led to massive layoffs, huge unemployment, recession and economic devastation in America's manufacturing heartland - the Rust Belt: Michigan, Wisconsin, Indiana, Illinois, Ohio, and Pennsylvania. Formerly hardcore Democratic or blue states are now in play in this presidential election as a result of the Brexit-like revolt of the American working and middle income classes.

Similarly in England's industrial heartland - the industrial towns and cities in the north of England, the onetime stronghold of the leftist Labour party - voted overwhelmingly to leave the European Union.

What we are seeing is the revenge of the working and middle classes of the UK and the United States uniting to turf out whom they believe to be the engineers of their economic downfall.

Workers of the industrial heartland unite! You have nothing to lose but being chained to Cameron, Corbyn and the pantsuited Hillary. Ha Ha!

Hillary and her overpaid legions of spinmeisters will try to spin that what happened in Brexit stays in Brexit.

But she is just Queen Canute, delusional in her fruitless efforts to turn back the tide of history and the onrushing tide of the future.

I predict Hillary will be swamped by American exiteers who want Hillary and her band of clueless, myopic liberal elitist social warriors - who are and have always been contemptuous of and indifferent to the plight of average American working men and women regardless of race, creed, color or ethnicity - to exit once and for all from the American political scene. To make room for the Trumpster, the orange-haired populist who at least understands them, gets them and recognizes their pain.

July 2, 2016

Hey, Donald! Choose Newton 4 VP and Defy Political Gravity

* * * * * * * * * * * * *

Anything is possible with Donald Trump. He is consistently unpredictable, always going against the political grain. Marching to his own drummer. Making up his own rules as he goes along and then not following his own rules.

But underneath the bombast and blarney, Trump is a clear-eyed, cold-hearted, calculating realist.

He knows that his strengths are his acute political instincts. He has an innate ability to perceive "the big picture", but a "big picture" that is usually a very different picture than is portrayed by the mainstream media.

While such unimaginative liberal politicians as Obama and Hillary were extolling the virtues of Britain staying within the EU and fully expecting that Britain would ultimately vote to stay, Trump brilliantly saw and understood the greater picture - that there was a much more powerful populist, nationalistic, anti-elitist, pro-Britain-for-Britons story in play. Contrary to the slow-thinking Obama and Hillary, Trump predicted the Brexit side would triumph. Which it did - decisively and with a vengeance.

Other Trumpian strengths are his fearlessness and courage to question and ridicule convention, conventional politicians and conventional political opinions.

Trump brilliantly intuited his opponents' weaknesses and called them out on them, i.e. Ted Cruz, Marco Rubio, the very weak Jeb Bush and cowardly Mittens Romney.

Trump has no political experience in comparison to Hillary, who has been in public life, for better or worse (mostly worse, in my humble opinion) for several decades. Hillary has out-fundraised and out-organized Trump on the ground. Hillary, her PACS and pack animals have spent millions and millions of dollars trying vainly to deliver a fatal blow to Trump's presidential chances.

Notwithstanding all of the above, and despite Hillary being abetted by the mainstream press, Trump has driven the political agenda for the last six months. Hillary knows it. Her lackeys know it and the American people know it.

According to a recent Quinnipiac poll, the majority of American people believe that Trump - this very well known self-promoting real estate developer and bombastic reality television host - could better manage the economy and fight terrorism than Hillary. Many Americans may not like Trump, but clearly the majority of Americans do not trust Hillary.

Even Hillary's major supporters and defenders agree that she is not very likeable, but she has tons of political experience. Whereas Trump has nil, nada, zip, gornicht. And his lack of political experience and knowledge of the nitty gritty of Washington lawmaking makes many Americans nervous.

Therefore Newt Gingrich is Trump's obvious choice for vice president.

Newt was an elected congressman for twenty years from the sixth district of Georgia. In 1995 he led the GOP party to majority control of the House of Representatives for the first time in four decades and he ascended to Speaker of the House. Prior to running for Congress, Newt, who has a Ph.D in History, was a university professor. He has authored and co-authored twenty-seven books. His knowledge of Europe and Asia is encyclopedic.

As noted, in the '90s Newt was the congressional head of the Republicans. As Speaker of the House, he knows how to get things done as a politico insider. In the mid '90s he helped bring about welfare reform and the reduction of the capital gains tax. Newt also knows how to be a rabble rouser, an outlier and to stir up shite, organize political opposition and block legislation or policies unappealing to him and the Republican party. As Newt effectively did in the '90s when Hillary, acting as Bill Clinton's health care adviser, tried to promote her health care system. And failed miserably, thanks in part to Newt's tenacious adversarial efforts.

Newt was also a leading political force in Washington pushing for Slick Willy's impeachment for lying to Congress and the American people that he did not have sexual relations with his innocent, naïve and victimized female intern, Monica Lewinsky.

So Newt also has a hard-on against the Clintons and has been a burr under their bonnets for decades and has tons of political experience in the Congressional trenches.

All music to Trump's ears.

Make no mistake - Newt is no choir boy. He has his personal flaws and defects. He has had and will have his issues. A wife or three. Some scandalous extramarital affairs under his belt. But then who doesn't have a few skeletons in the closet? A few things in our past, of which we are not proud.

Newt has great political instincts. And to his credit he had the cojones to come out for Trump publicly, articulately and persuasively, well before Trump secured the GOP nomination.

And most importantly, Trump and Newt get along – a very critical element to any successful president/VP ticket.

The Newt will be nominated by Trump within days, well before the GOP convention. With Newt in his corner, Trump will be better able to argue that he has covered off his lack of Washington political experience.

There is a very smart, bright, competent and experienced political hand on the rudder with Captain Trump.

The Donald and The Newt will be a formidable dynamic duo.

"Between the parental generation shaped by the Depression and World War II and their 1960s middle-class offspring, the world sometimes seemed to have broken in two. Between the church-oriented and nonviolent black civil rights activists of the South and the later ghetto revolutionists of the North rose another fatal hiatus. Between the Vietnam "hawks" and "doves" lay a subterranean abyss that threatened the fabric of civilized debate, even of society itself, in an America enervated and splintered more than any period since the Civil War: black versus white, rich versus poor, urban versus suburban, a balkanization of emotions and fealties and dependencies. And there were about two dozen other chasms, political, social, cultural, rivaling themselves in wildness and acridity."

- Willie Morris, *New York Days*, 1993

PART THREE:

AMERICA IN TURMOIL

TRUMP WANTS TO MAKE AMERICA SAFE AGAIN - FROM THE CLINTONS

July 3, 2016

Will Shakespeare "Outs" Hillary in "Comedy of Errors"

✶ ✶ ✶ ✶ ✶ ✶ ✶ ✶ ✶ ✶ ✶ ✶ ✶

Recently I took in Shakespeare's "The Comedy of Errors," performed as part of the Toronto Fringe Festival, a performance that took place on the second floor of the infamous Victory Café.

I have not read "The Comedy of Errors" since I studied "Hum 7" (Humanities 7), a general survey theatre course in my undergraduate Harvard days, BI (Before Internet.)

When I reread the play prior to the performance I was not that interested in the two major characters: Two sets of identical brothers, both separated at a very early age from each other and from their parents.

It is a brilliant concept and the basis for a play of mistaken identities, as both the older nobler identical twins have the same name - Antipholus - and their respective man servants (who are also identical fraternal twins) both answer to the name Dromio.

It's great farcical fun, as all the characters are confused for one another while the main characters think the townspeople are stark raving mad and the locals think the major characters are lunatics as well.

But what is more interesting to me is the Bard's complex and modern view of marriage, women and a woman's place in society, especially as embodied in the fascinating Adriana, the wife of Antipholus from Ephesus (as opposed to Antipholus from Syracuse.)

Adriana is married to a military hero, a successful and apparently wealthy businessman, prominent in society, who also has the support of Solinus, the Duke of Ephesus, the most powerful man in the country.

Accordingly, Adriana lives in a very large house and has several male and female servants to attend to her every whim. Sort of *Downton Abbey*, 16th century style.

But all is not hunky dory in the House of Antipholus. In this case, money, political power and social prominence do not buy marital bliss or even happiness.

Adriana's husband also seems to be a philanderer - a rake, who enjoys the company of the courtesan who owns the local tavern. Shades of Bill and Hillary Clinton.

This state of affairs (literally) makes Adriana positively ballistic – and rightfully so.

Adriana is depicted as a very strong, independent, intelligent, passionate and proud woman. Think Elizabeth Bennet of *Pride and Prejudice* or Lady Mary of *Downton Abbey*. And of course, the unsinkable and nearly indictable Hillary.

In speaking to her more compliant sister Luciana (still unwed), Adriana criticizes the double standard in her society, in which men have much more freedom than women to fool around. *("Why should their liberty than ours be more?")*

Adriana clearly loves her husband, but is also very angry with his playing around. And she is frustrated that society apparently condones her husband's behavior and frowns on Adriana's public display of anger and disappointment with her husband. On the other hand, Adriana astutely observes that her husband and society would condemn her if she, too, took a lover.

In one of the most powerful speeches in the play, Adriana anticipates her husband's violent reaction, if the roles were reversed:

> *"How dearly would it touch you to the quick,*
> *Shouldst thou but hear I were licentious?...*
> *Wouldst thou not spit at me, and spurn at me,*
> *And hurl the name of husband in my face,*
> *And tear the stain'd skin off my harlot brow,*
> *And from my false hand, cut the wedding-ring,*
> *And break it with a deep-divorcing vow?"*

It seems what is true in 16th century England, is still true to this day. Recall that Bubba "Horn Dog" Clinton had a plethora of beautiful bimbos at his beck and call while Arkansas governor.

And I doubt Monica Lewinsky was the first and last female who serviced Clinton at his pleasure in the Oval Office.

Still Clinton survived as a two term President, retained his marriage, and is still revered as a great President. He is now internationally respected as a very wealthy and powerful speaker and philanthropist.

Could you imagine if the lovely Hillary, while First Lady, was caught between the sheets doing the horizontal tango with a hot male Secret Service agent?

There would have been Hill to pay.

I think Bill would have dropped Hillary like a hot tamale.

There would not have been a second or third act for the disgraced Hillary.

Recall when Maggie Trudeau, Prime Minister Justin's flaky hippie mom, was publicly exposed (literally) doing the Rolling Stones at a famous Toronto bar, the El Mocambo; Trudeau Sr., to use the above Bard's words, permanently terminated the marriage and "tore the stained skin off of that licentious harlot's brow, and from her false hand, cut the wedding-ring and broke it with a deep divorcing vow."

So how does Shakespeare explain the double standard afflicting women in 16th century England?

According to Luciana in "The Comedy of Errors", Adriana's younger unwed sister, men are superior and can get away with lots of crap, because it is the natural order of things:

> *"The beasts, the fishes, and the winged fowls*
> *Are their males' subjects, and at their controls;*
> *Man, more divine, the master of all these,*
> *Lord of the wide world and wild wat'ry seas,*
> *Indued with intellectual sense and souls,*
> *Of more pre-eminence than fish and fowls,*
> *Are masters to their females, and the lords."*

So let us fast forward to the present time.

Mankind is still the master of "beasts, fishes and winged fowl," but then again so is womankind.

And science, biology, history, experience and Donald Trump have shown us that man is no more divine than woman. And clearly no more imbued with intellectual sense and soul. In fact, it is arguable that many of us poor schmucks are imbued with a lot less intelligence and common sense.

And hence, we men have no legitimate claim to being masters of our females.

Luciana thought men were also superior because, unlike women, tied to the house and home and relegated to household chores, "men's business still lies out o'door."

But that clearly no longer applies in today's modern society.

Modern women are no longer tied to hearth and home.

Women these days are much more financially independent. The majority are career women: Captains of industry, lawyers, doctors, accountants, consultants, teachers, social workers, civil servants, business people, white and blue collar workers and - let us not forget - high-powered and powerful politicians.

Adriana thought her cheating, roguish husband was:

> *"Deformed, crooked, old and sere,*
> *Vicious, ungentle, foolish, blunt, unkind"*

But notwithstanding the above, Adriana, came to her husband's aid when he was wrongfully put in jail.

Why did Adriana stand by her man?

Perhaps there was still some love, but the more

reasonable answer, was in those days and in that situation, Adriana, without her husband, would have been left with no wealth, no home, no servants, no social standing. Her life and situation would have been considerably worse. Especially far from her comfortable home.

> *"And yet would herein others' eyes were worse,*
> *Far from her nest the lapwing cries away."*

But Hillary?

Why did she stick by her man?

After Bill completed his presidency, Hillary could have dumped his sorry ass. She was well known, a lawyer and very well respected and connected. She had the financial means to successfully separate from Bill.

But I believe she made the practical and political calculation that staying with Bill, a more powerful and more popular public figure than herself, would be better for her politically in terms of a potential run for the Senate - or even the presidency.

History has proven Hillary to be correct in that calculation.

I think the Bard would be very amused looking at Hillary today through Adriana's eyes. I suspect the Bard may conclude that though women have come a long way, baby, they still have a long way to go.

July 9, 2016

Black Lives Matter Disrupts Toronto Gay Pride Parade: Have They Gone Friggin Looney Tunes?

* * * * * * * * * * * * *

Recently members of Black Lives Matter (BLM) Toronto, which had been honored guests of Toronto's annual Pride Parade in downtown Toronto, hijacked the very festival that had included them with a sit-in. This bunch of predominantly black and aboriginal thugs threatened to wreck a joyous event that had drawn a huge number of LGBTQ and non-LGBTQ people from Toronto, Ontario and the rest of Canada to this fabulous parade of hope, love, diversity and inclusiveness - unless the organizers of Pride agreed to its set of extortionate demands on the spot.

BLM's most egregious demand was to prevent the future involvement of gay and non gay police officers in the Pride Parade, because these disgusting lowlifes believed the Toronto police (headed, by the way, by a black chief of police) engaged in police brutality. Their very presence, they alleged, made the black LGBTQ members feel they "were not in a safe place."

In order to permit the Parade to proceed (it was a very hot day and hundreds of thousands were in attendance) the organizers caved to these extortionate demands. A day later, the chairman of Pride rightfully disavowed signing such a disgusting document under duress.

BLM Toronto thought they won a political victory. In reality, they got shite. They incurred the wrath of the majority of liberal and conservative Torontonians who believe the rule of law should take precedent over thuggery and criminality masquerading as quick political fixes. The sad fact is that BLM is representative of a Toronto black community that has marginalized itself.

Black Lives Matter, together with the most outspoken members of the Toronto black community, believe that the reason the black community is still by and large on the lowest rung of Toronto's socio-economic ladder (together with the aboriginal community) is due to external forces: White privilege, structural and institutional racism, British colonialism. Blah, blah, blah. blah. It is always society's fault. Or history's fault. Or slavery over 150 years ago. To the black community and these pathetic leaders, it has nothing to do with the black community itself or its own culture.

The fact is Toronto is a city of immigrants who have all faced prejudice in their lives or the lives of their grandparents and parents: Italians, Greeks, Irish, South

Asians, Asians, Japanese, Jews, Koreans, Filipinos, Vietnamese, Ismailis, to name a few. Many such groups faced racial prejudice due to their color. Others due to being foreign and unable to properly communicate in English.

But all these groups, notwithstanding enormous prejudice, racism or xenophobia, are flourishing and prospering in Toronto and to a large extent have surpassed the still struggling black community.

Because all these groups took responsibility for their own community and their own community members and for themselves. They did not whine and beat their breasts and blame society for their unfortunate situation.

These groups to a large extent emphasized hard work, education and strong family units. Most of these groups were shunned by the majority culture, so they built communities from within. They built local businesses, community centres and institutions that catered to the interests of these groups. They worked hard. They sacrificed for their children and they fought to have their children go to school, stay in school and go on to university and grad school and rise up in Toronto socio-economic society on merit, grit, determination and smarts. The downtown campus of University of Toronto is full of second- and third-generation Asians, South Asians, Koreans, Persians, Filipinos and more, studying to be bankers, accountants, engineers, lawyers, doctors, consultants, businessmen and the like.

These newer immigrant groups as the older immigrant groups are rising in Toronto society in business, in politics and in the community.

These groups are not looking for the quick fix. Or the quick and easy score. Or in the case of Black Lives Matter, the quick and easy political fix by hijacking Pride. That is not the difficult political organizing which leads ultimately to enduring and durable political power. It is just a quick political score. BLM will go the way of other faddish and forgettable political activist groups like Occupy Toronto, or Occupy Wall Street or Idle No More.

It is about time that the real leaders of the black community stand up and be counted and take responsibility for the ills of their black society and black culture. Most of the homicides in Toronto are black men killing black men.

Police are not killing black men. Black men are killing black men. Stop using racism as a cop out. (No pun intended). There are serious problems that the real black leadership should be addressing from within the community and fixing from within the community. Instead of relying on the quick and temporary fixes of such reviled groups as the thuggish Black Lives Matter.

July 12, 2016

Crime and Protests in the Streets: It's 1968 All Over Again

Crooked, lying Hillary, the most untrustworthy Democratic candidate in modern times, thought she had the American presidency all locked up about a week ago. She had Obama campaigning for her with his great support in the black and Hispanic communities. Hillary thought that notwithstanding all the terrible political baggage she and Slick Willy have been carrying for decades, she would easily defeat the political novice, the controversial Donald Trump.

That is, until Obama came out of his shell in the wake of the tragic killings of two black men by cops and publicly criticized the American police for being racist, explicitly supporting the black militant, anti-white, anti-police Black Lives Matter folks, who during their public protests were calling for the killing of "the racist white pigs."

Unfortunately for Obama, Obama conveniently forgot to publicly criticize the anti-white and anti-cop ravings of Black Lives Matter. Obama, playing to the politically correct liberal media, failed to point out that 90 per cent of black killings were the result of black on black murders. Not white police. Not white American citizens.

And not because of institutional racism.

How are black on black killings a result of white racism?

Hillary, seeing no downside to following Obama's lead, echoed Obama's sentiments and also came down on so-called racist white cops for blatantly killing innocent black men.

Obama, thinking that he secured his legacy of being supportive of black people against the evil racist police, took off to Europe.

Then the Dallas massacre happened

A black militant dude, a former Army veteran, with premeditation and enormous preparation, calmly and cold-bloodedly killed five Dallas cops who were keeping the peace at a supposedly peaceful Black Lives Matter protest rally.

The shooter, Micah Johnson, declared for all to hear that he was influenced by Black Lives Matter's anti-white and anti-cop rhetoric. He declared that he wanted to kill white people and specifically white cops. Implicitly, he was influenced by Obama/Hillary's pro antiracist cop rhetoric.

Then the social media shite really hit the fan. Republican senators, congressmen and conservative pundits came down heavy on Obama and Hillary for influencing this black cop killer and in effect inciting a race war between blacks and white police.

Poor Obama was stranded in Europe with his anti-white and anti-cop rhetoric. No matter how hard he and his White House and liberal media tried, he was caught out - exposed as sympathetic to cop killing black militants.

And of course Hillary, who had hitched her political career to Obama, was also caught with her signature pantsuit down.

Then Trump, against all expectations, came out with a rational and reasoned prepared statement where he sympathized with the deaths of the black men and the five Dallas cops gunned down and their respective families, and declared himself the law and order candidate who was - and has always - been pro-cop and pro-law and order.

And that he would do all he could as President to protect all American people regardless of race, color or creed.

Trump's message has resonated throughout America, especially in those vulnerable communities, where gangs, drugs and killings run rampant.

I predict that if Trump stays on message (which is, of course, never a given) - especially with the law and order message that resonates with men and women and all the minority groups, including the black and Hispanic communities - Trump will triumph over the seemingly anti-cop, pro-BLM Hillary in November.

July 12, 2016

The Blood of 5 Murdered Dallas Cops Finally Sticks to Teflon Barry

* * * * * * * * * * * * *

(NOTE: As of July 17, 2016, three more policemen have been gunned down in Baton Rouge, Louisiana. The head of the Cleveland police association accused Barack Obama of having blood on his hands for these most recent killings, for apparently supporting the views of Black Lives Matter, who are calling for violence against police officers. His comments are very similar to my observations below, in the wake of the killing of five policemen by a black militant, influenced by Black Lives Matter and, effectively, the words of Obama.)

To paraphrase the words of FBI Chief Comey, President Obama and Hillary Clinton did not explicitly intend that their public support of the anti-police, anti-white, black militant group Black Lives Matter should cause the cowardly killing of five Dallas cops by a black militant.

But in the case of Hillary, she was very careless and even negligent in her blanket condemnation of police and white people. As a result, Hillary knew - or should have known -

her words would influence some cowardly black militant to hunt down and kill five Dallas policemen, who were just doing their job protecting American citizens.

Barack Obama is another story.

He is the consummate orator and wordsmith. I strongly believe that Obama knew exactly what he was saying and knew deep down in his heart that his words - his public condemnation of racist white police who had killed unarmed black men - would have the intended effect that it did. Obama's words gave support to Micah Xavier Johnson, a 25-year-old black Army veteran who, with premeditation and considerable preparation, went out as a trained sniper and cold-bloodedly killed five unprotected Dallas police officers, injuring several other officers.

Let me elaborate on this argument. Because the circumstantial evidence against Obama is overwhelming and has been hiding in plain sight.

Recall when Obama first ran for election as president in 2008 and promised that by electing him, America will once and for all move past its racist history, and evolve into a potentially post-racial and peaceful country. Recall Obama also ran on the "Hope and Change" ticket promising to be above partisan politics. To Obama there were no "red" states (Republican) or "blue" states (Democratic), but just the unified United States, implying that he would also unify the country and through his example he would lead the US into a post-partisan era.

As to the latter part, Obama has failed miserably. The country has been seriously divided during Obama's two terms between the Democrats and the GOP in Congress and throughout the land. I argue that his very presidency, his aloof/arrogant character, his confrontational hectoring manner and his highly partisan approach to governance have further divided the country.

As to the first part Obama - America's first black president - America's great white hope and change president - has also failed miserably in bridging the divide between white America and black America. As a result of the worst black shootings of white cops in America's history, I argue that America is returning to the horrible 1960s where whites and blacks were at each other's throats. Police and black protesters (Black Lives Matter and others) battle each other in the streets. Obama must take some responsibility for this horrible state of affairs.

For the most part during Obama's first term and part of his second term, Obama eschewed pontificating from his presidential bully pulpit about what he believed to be the ongoing racial divide between black and white America.

But now in his last year, unshackled by concerns of re-election, more interested in his legacy - which requires Obama to actively support the flawed campaign and heavily flawed character of Hillary by energizing his black American base - he has finally exposed his true nature.

In his heart and soul, Obama has a great deal of sympathy for militant groups like Black Lives Matter, which is in essence an anti-white, anti-cop, black power militant group that views violence against police and white people as a reasonable and justifiable solution, similar to the Nation of Islam militants and the violent Black Panthers of the '60s and '70s.

Donald Trump, who has great natural gifts of intuition and political instinct, was perfectly correct when he suggested (and he has been suggesting this for years publicly and on social media) there is something wrong with Obama. There is just something "off" about the man. Obama is not really what he seems. There is something hidden underneath his oh-so-cool exterior, his aloof and intellectually superior demeanor.

Something anti-American about Obama.

Trump was not only referring to the obvious fact that Obama, notwithstanding his protestations to the contrary, clearly has sympathy for radical Muslims, but that Obama also has sympathy for anti-American black power militants like Black Lives Matter.

This conclusion should not come as any surprise to anyone who has followed Obama's life very closely.

For example, Obama's own autobiography, *Dreams from My Father*, provides a telling clue to the essence of Obama.

In a very revealing memory of his youth, as a high school senior, searching for his true identity as a black man,

Obama talks about certain black role models (pages 85-86.)

He seemingly discards the example of W.E.B. Dubois, a well-known black academic, writer and intellectual who stressed education and peaceful integration into the greater white society as a possible means for the American black community to achieve real political power within the greater white American society.

Instead, Obama during this pivotal time of self-discovery seemed to be most influenced by the teachings of the Muslim black power militant, Malcolm X.

Obama writes:

> *"I had begun to see a new map of the world, one that was frightening in its simplicity, suffocating in its implications. We were always playing on the white man's court... by the white man's rules. If the principal, or the coach, or a teacher, or Kurt, wanted to spit in your face, he could because he had the power and you didn't. If he decided not to, if he treated you like a man or came to your defense, it was because he knew that the words you spoke, the clothes you wore, the books you read, your ambitions and desires, were already his. Whatever he decided to do, it was his decision to make, not yours, and because of that fundamental power he held over you, because it preceded and would outlast his individual motives and inclinations, any distinction between good and bad whites held negligible meaning."*

"In fact, you couldn't even be sure that everything you had assumed to be an expression of your black, unfettered self - the humor, the song, the behind-the-back pass - had been freely chosen for you. At best, these things were a refuge; at worst, a trap."

"Following this maddening logic, the only thing you could choose as your own was withdrawal into a smaller and smaller coil of rage, until being black meant only the knowledge of your own powerlessness, of your own defeat. And the final irony: Should you refuse this defeat and lash out at your captors, they would have a name for that, too, a name that could cage you just as good. Paranoid, Militant. Violent. Nigger."

"...Even DuBois's learning and Baldwin's love and Langston's humour, eventually succumbed to its corrosive force."

(**Note:** Obama is referring to "the same anguish, the same doubt; a self-contempt" of being a powerless black man in a white racist society.")

But then Obama has a revelation. He continues:

"Only Malcolm X's autobiography seemed to offer something different. His repeated acts of self-creation spoke to me; the blunt poetry of his words, his unadorned insistence on respect, promised a new and uncompromising order, martial in its discipline, forged through sheer force of will. All the other stuff, the talk of

blue-eyed devils and apocalypse, was incidental to that program...And yet, even as I imagined myself following Malcolm's call, one line in the book stayed with me. He spoke of a wish he'd once had, the wish that the white blood that ran through him, there by an act of violence, might somehow be expunged."

Malcolm X was the anti-Martin Luther King. Whereas King preached peaceful protest, civil disobedience and black integration into the greater white society, Malcolm X preached about black power, black supremacy, black separateness. Ideally, forming a black separate nation within the United States, aptly called The Nation of Islam. And Malcolm X preached and supported black people standing up for themselves against the racist white American society and engaging in violence, if necessary.

Read, watch and listen closely to how the current Black Lives Matter movement resonates with Malcolm X's anti-white hatred, black power, black supremacy, and support of black violence and protest, if necessary.

It is no coincidence that Obama, influenced by Malcolm X's provocative teachings, is similarly supportive of the extremist/militant views and black power ideology of Black Lives Matter.

After his murder in 1965 the ghost of Malcolm X was at the forefront of black militancy. Before his assassination he was the second-in-command of an essentially anti-white, anti-American organization called the Nation of Islam. A very attractive strong black organization which obviously resonated for Obama as a young, fatherless, half white/half black man, looking for answers and searching for his identity.

Similarly, Obama spent twenty years in the congregation of another controversial pastor, Pastor Jeremiah Wright, whose sermons were frequently laced with anti-white and anti-American rhetoric.

Do you remember when Wright preached, post-9/11, that the radical Islamic terror leveled on New York in which over 3,000 Americans died was a result of American imperialistic power, and as a result America got what it had deserved? According to Wright, Obama's pastor for over twenty years, the chickens have come home to roost.

Specifically, Wright preached in public to Obama and his wife, Michelle:

> *"We bombed Hiroshima, we bombed Nagasaki, and we nuked far more than the thousands in New York and the Pentagon, and we never batted an eye... and now we are indignant, because the stuff we have done overseas is now brought back into our own front yards. America's chickens are coming home to roost."*

This is a portion of Wright's infamous *"God and Governments"* sermon that was aired on all the major media around the time of Obama's race against Hillary Clinton in the Democratic primaries in 2008:

"When it came to treating her citizens of African descent fairly, America failed. She put them in chains, the government put them on slave quarters, put them on auction blocks, put them in cotton fields, put them in inferior schools, put them in substandard housing, put them in scientific experiments, put them in the lowest paying jobs, put them outside the equal protection of the law, kept them out of their racist bastions of higher education and locked them into positions of hopelessness and helplessness. The government gives them the drugs, builds bigger prisons, passes a three-strike law and then wants us to sing 'God Bless America.' No, no, no, not God Bless America. God damn America — that's in the Bible — for killing innocent people. God damn America, for treating our citizens as less than human. God damn America, as long as she tries to act like she is God, and she is supreme. The United States government has failed the vast majority of her citizens of African descent."

Barack Obama, with his wife Michele by his side, listened to this anti-American and anti-white ranting and raving for over twenty years in Pastor Wright's Trinity United Church of Christ in Chicago. Clearly, Obama found comfort and validation in Wright's teachings and sermons (which echoed Malcolm X's diatribes against white and imperialistic America) or Obama would have left his church many years prior to his departure, for political reasons. His association with Wright and his church were hurting his chances of beating Hillary in the 2008 Democratic presidential race.

Even Hillary called out Obama in 2008 for seeming to support Wright's views as Hillary noted, "You don't choose your family, but you choose what church you want to attend." The fact that Obama considered Wright as his moral and religious leader, notwithstanding Wright's anti-white and unpatriotic fiery speeches, speaks volumes about Obama's true intentions and his true feelings about America, race and the treatment of the black community by white America.

Immediately following the shootings of two black men by two white police in Louisiana and Minnesota, speaking in Europe, Obama blamed these two white cops for murder prior to the conclusion of any investigation. So much for the presumption of innocence until being proven guilty.

But Obama did not stop there. He blamed not only these two cops, but the whole U.S. criminal justice system.

Just after offering his condolences to the families of the victims, Alton Sterling and Philando Castle, Obama stated bluntly the following:

> *"All of us as Americans should be troubled by these shootings because these are not isolated incidents…They're symptomatic of a broader set of racial disparities that exist in our criminal justice system…The data shows black folks are more vulnerable to these kinds of incidents…. We have seen tragedies like this too many times."*

"There's a big chunk of our fellow citizenry that feels as if because the color of their skin they're not being treated the same. And that hurts. And that should trouble all of us."

"Obama concluded that criminal justice legislation is necessary to address racial biases "that have to be rooted out" but has stalled amid election-year politics. "This should be a spur to action to get that done."

What Obama did not do and what he should have done as a black President was rebuke Black Lives Matter for conveniently ignoring the thousands of black-on-black killings, especially in Chicago - Obama's home town and America's Murder Capital. How are all these black-on-black killings the result of racist white cops? They are not. Obama should have called for greater black personal and community responsibility to combat black on black killings. He did not. He pushed the Black Lives Matter lie that all black deaths are the result of white racism.

Simply, according to Obama (and Hillary who is desperately clinging to Obama's coat tails in order to benefit from Obama's obvious black community support) the whole American criminal justice system is shot through with institutional racism and racial disparities as a result of two white cops allegedly murdering two black dudes.

It follows using this Obama logic that all American society is shot through with such institutional racism.

Which should be rooted out. Action is required.

Obama knew exactly what he was saying and doing. He was calling for action. For revenge against the black killings by white cops.

Within hours of Obama calling for action against white cops, Micah Johsnon took out his registered rifle and, influenced by BLM and Obama's well-publicized comments, struck a blow for anti-white black hatred and revenge and murdered five policemen in cold blood, ironically while they were protecting a BLM rally in Dallas.

In this case, Obama's words had the intended effect. Johnson listened to Obama who blamed white cops and the whole white society for the deaths of those unfortunate black men. And Obama called for action to root out this white racism. So Johnson went out and killed white men - white cops.

Shame on Black Lives Matter.

Shame on Barack Hussein Obama II.

July 13, 2016

The Obama Years Revisited: All White Liberal Lies Matter

★ ★ ★ ★ ★ ★ ★ ★ ★ ★ ★ ★ ★

My good friend Gerald, in a very good Facebook post, reminded me of the many failings of the Nixon Administration. Among the many things he criticized Nixon for was Nixon's failure to follow his predecessor Lyndon B. Johnson's withdrawal program from Vietnam in the late '60s and '70s. As a student of history and government during that time, I had thought my friend had engaged in some typical revisionist liberal history. I remember that time differently. Here is my take on the '60s and the '70s as they resonate still today in the Obama era that is, fortunately, coming to an end, not with a bang but with a characteristic whimper.

LBJ was a great president in terms of passing historic bipartisan domestic legislation, i.e. the Civil Rights Act, Voters Rights Act, immigration reform and significant Great Society social reforms (Medicare and Medicaid) which all provided a necessary safety net for vulnerable and senior Americans.

Contrast that with Obama's inability, incompetence and inexperience in doing what was politically and legislatively necessary to pass his domestic legislation.

During the first two Obama years, the Democrats had majorities in the Senate and House of Reps. It is historically interesting to note that Obama had to resort to lies and misrepresentations in order to have passed his very complicated and flawed Obamacare. Recall Obama going on public television and lying to the American people by promising the American voters, that "you will not be forced to change your doctor or your insurance plan. "

History will show that Obama oversaw a failed presidency. It will show, for example, that he clearly lacked LBJ's superior wheeling and dealing abilities with both houses and on both sides of the aisle.

Perhaps the time is right for a return to the LBJ style of horse trading and bargaining between the parties, which produced such significant and enduring bipartisan legislation.

LBJ's major downfall was deploying thousands of American men to fight in the Vietnam War - with the active support of Kennedy liberals and Democrats, by the way, who said that America was fighting the spread of communism, when in fact it was essentially a local civil war.

LBJ did not seek re-election because the North Vietnamese demonstrated that the Americans had entered into a quagmire from which it could not emerge victorious. Also his own Democrats and the anti-war movement turned against LBJ in the 1968 presidential primaries. LBJ's approval rating went down also because of race riots and the feeling in America that the country needed a return to law and order and safety in the streets and in the cities. Is history repeating itself now?

(I suspect that the majority of Americans now are sick and tired of protesters flaunting the laws and illegally blocking their highways and byways and blaming them, hard-working Americans, for the ills of their society. Without these particular groups taking any individual or community responsibility for the obvious defects in their own culture and society. But I digress.)

For all of the above, LBJ did not seek re-election as president.

There is no evidence that LBJ had any intention of leaving Vietnam so quickly, because he did not stay around for a second term. So to blame Nixon for not following LBJ's non-existent withdrawal from the Vietnam War is a serious bit of revisionist liberal history.

Gerald, objective non-liberal historians have credited Nixon and Kissinger for managing a brilliant realpolitik American foreign policy, which always put America's interests first and brilliantly expanded American military and diplomatic power in the world and gave important military support and cover to America's allies.

Both Nixon and Kissinger were students of the famous Prussian theorist, Clausewitz, whose famous saying was, "War is the continuation of politics (policy) by other means."

It is too bad Obama never studied Clausewitz, or Nixon/Kissinger for that matter. Perhaps if he had, Obama would not have so thoroughly undermined America's stature and power in the world.

Recall when Obama as Commander-in-Chief and supposedly the most powerful guy in the world, representing the only real global superpower, threatened Syrian President Assad with severe military consequences if Assad crossed the "red line" and chemically gassed his own people. Assad did. The American western allies were prepared to bomb Assad and punish him. Obama blinked. Did nothing. America's allies were shocked at Obama and America's weakness and cowardice. Putin, seeking an advantage, stepped in, and now Russia is a major power in the Middle East.

And European and Asian allies think Obama is a spineless wimp. An international laughingstock. An unreliable international leader and ally. And America, a toothless tiger.

So much for America's traditional and historical exceptionalism.

Recall when Obama recently went to Britain and implored Britons to stay in the EU, Boris Johnson ridiculed Obama as the son of an anti-British colonist and anti-imperialist Kenyan. This is one of the most astute and damning critiques of Obama's flawed character and his flawed presidency. Boris's criticism explains brilliantly why Obama embarked on so many international apology tours. He was embarrassed about the previous exercise of American military power. As an American president! How crazy is that? Obama thought and thinks that by sucking up and appeasing radical Muslim terrorists, they won't commit terrorism against Americans. Now that is dangerous and stupid thinking!

Oh, by the way, the Britons voted overwhelmingly to ignore Obama's empty rhetoric and Brexit won.

Getting back to Nixon/Kissinger. Contrast the situation in the 70s that Nixon/Kissinger faced.

Recall that in those days, the Soviet Union was a superpower that had major influence in Eastern Europe, the Middle East, in Africa, Cuba, parts of Latin America and South America and China was emerging as a superpower in the East. Nixon and Kissinger assumed a bad hand in Vietnam which was the product of Kennedy and LBJ's stupid adventurism, but unlike Obama, Nixon/Kissinger did not cut and run and undermine America's position and power in the world as a superpower, to be feared and respected.

Nixon/Kissinger knew what the incompetent Obama never figured out - that diplomacy can only be successful if it is backed up by hard and massive military power. Otherwise, American diplomacy is just meaningless and ineffectual rhetoric.

Or as the two Williams – Shakespeare and Faulkner – would say, "sound and fury, signifying nothing, told by an idiot."

Accordingly, Nixon/Kissinger stayed in Vietnam and in Southeast Asia, admittedly at great loss of life and treasure, to maintain America's credibility and military deterrent power in a very dangerous world. But for Nixon/Kissinger's very real and hard military power and deterrent power, Russia and its Russian-backed Arab allies may not have been deterred by American support of Israel during the 1973 Yom Kippur War. And instead Russia and its Arab allies might have killed hundreds of thousands of Israeli Jews in the process.

Nixon the anti-communist is also noteworthy for leading America to recognize Communist Red China, something that the Democratic Kennedy and LBJ failed to do. Nixon did this to brilliantly play China off the then very formidable Soviet Union.

As to Watergate and its cover up, there is no question that Nixon fracked up and impeded the investigation and was going to be impeached in the Senate so he resigned in disgrace. But Gerald my friend, at least in the Watergate matter there was an independent special prosecutor investigating Republican government officials who had clearly obstructed justice.

Contrast that with the corrupt way the Obama Administration handled the investigation of Hillary Clinton for allegedly violating the Espionage Act by being grossly negligent by being in possession of government documents relating to national defense outside of the secure custody of the government.

Where was the special prosecutor in this case?

Especially because many in the US Justice Department were conflicted Bill Clinton appointees and Clinton loyalists.

While the State Department and the FBI were investigating Hillary Clinton, Obama prejudiced the investigation several times by publicly stating that Hillary may have been careless, but no national secrets were revealed. Therefore, she broke no laws.

Could you imagine if Nixon publicly stated, while the FBI were investigating his aides Haldeman and Ehrlichman, that he had exonerated them and in effect influenced the final disposition of these two. As Obama apparently did in the case of Hillary.

First of all, Obama should not have intervened. Secondly, Obama lied to the American public again.

FBI director James Comey concluded that Hillary's unsecure BlackBerry was probably hacked while she was in China or Russia, unfriendly countries. So it is very probable that Hillary disclosed through her gross negligence important American policies, plans and secrets that undermined America's national security interests.

Then you have Attorney General Loretta Lynch, who is overseeing the investigation of Hillary, meeting with Bill Clinton in a secret meeting in her airplane off the books and unrecorded. And Lynch failed to disclose this meeting until it was leaked to the press.

Apparently, Hillary Clinton has offered to renew Lynch's appointment as Attorney General if she is elected President.

There has been deceit, corruption and sleaziness by Obama and his administration on this toxic Hillary file.

Gerald, in the old days the biased liberal press would hide the corruption of Hillary, Obama and his whole administration as they hid Kennedy having numerous extra-marital affairs while President.

Fortunately, we have a vibrant, free, democratic and conservative online press and blogs to set the record straight about Obama and his failed and corrupt presidency.

Today, all white liberal lies matter.

July 14, 2016

Trump Surges Past Hillary in Three Key Swing States (THIS AINT NO JOKE!)

✶ ✶ ✶ ✶ ✶ ✶ ✶ ✶ ✶ ✶ ✶ ✶ ✶

The very well-respected Quinnipiac University poll came out with a poll yesterday that has three key swing states - Ohio, Pennsylvania and Florida - turning to Trump. What the frack?

Ohio: Trump-41 vs. Hillary-41
Florida: Trump-42 vs. Hillary-39
Pennsylvania: Trump-43 vs. Hillary-41

Note that no presidential candidate has won the presidency since 1960 without winning two of these three swing states.

Is this the end of Hillary?

I thought Hillary was political toast as soon as Trump won his first GOP primary in New Hampshire, in February, 2016.

Oftentimes, I feel that I am the goddess Cassandra. No, no, I am not transgendering a la Olympic superstar, Bruce Jenner. Though I personally think there is nothing wrong with that.

It is just not my thing.

More specifically, I am referring to the curse laid upon the poor goddess Cassandra who was fated to forever foretell the future, but never to be believed.

I sometimes feel that way. In February of 2016, when Trump first won the New Hampshire GOP primary, I predicted that Trump would not only win the GOP primaries, but that he would crush Bernie.

Okay, my powers failed me on that one. I thought the FBI would recommend indicting Hillary for violating the Espionage Act and Bernie would be the Democratic nominee by default. I overestimated the independence and integrity of the FBI chief and his people. I thought the FBI chief would do the honorable thing and recommend indictment. An indictment is being charged criminally. Not convicted. Hillary may have skated ultimately at trial. But such an indictment against the Hillary would have torpedoed the bad ship Hillary.

I still think Trump will crush Hillary by over 10 points nationally. The polls are catching up with me, but they are still underestimating the extent of Trump's popularity.

Because deep in my gut, I know these Trump supporters. Many of them are former Democrats. Many of them are highly educated professionals, business people, men and women from the affluent suburbs. Many are black, Hispanic, Asian, South Asian, Persian, Muslim. Many are keeping low to the ground. Not showing their true colors (pun intended.) Because it is politically incorrect in certain urban centres and college towns to be for Trump.

But his support is there. Quiet. Deep. Visceral. Solid. Very loyal.

The silent Trumpsters are not showing their true hand, until in the privacy of the polling booth. They will vote for Trump in overwhelming numbers. On election day in November, the silent but very deadly Trumpsters will crush Hillary's and Bill's dreams, once and for all.

These millions of Trump supporters will drive the proverbial stake in these politically vampirish, walking dead Clintons. Who have been sucking blood out of the American body politic for decades and decades.

Why has Trump surpassed Hillary?

The answers are obvious.

Since the last Quinnipiac poll, Hillary has dropped eight points.

She is losing because millions and millions of people do not trust her. They believe that she is an inveterate liar, who puts her personal interests above even American national security interests.

A majority of the American people believe Hillary should have been indicted for her alleged crimes in maintaining a private server and private email system outside the secure control and custody of the American government and for receiving and sending top security American documents through her unsecure BlackBerries, which probably were hacked by America's enemies.

And Hillary lied and lied and lied and lied some more about not sending and receiving Classified documents, even when they were marked "C." Hillary is not stupid. She is just a horrible, horrible person, whose every utterance is a lie. But this time her lies had national security implications.

And the American people have had it with Hillary and the slimy Slick Willy whose foundation received millions and millions of dollars from the worst Arab nations in the world while Hillary was Secretary of State.

The Arab sheiks and potentates did not send millions to Bill out of the goodness of their black hearts. They wanted influence. They wanted access. They wanted their interests protected by Hillary as one of the most powerful members of the Obama Administration.

And they got what they paid for.

The said Quinnipiac poll concludes as follows:

> *"By wide margins, voters in each state agree with the statement, 'The old way of doing things no longer works and we need radical change.' Voters also agree by wide margins that trade agreements with other countries have hurt them and their families' financial situation.*
>
> *"Voters still say Clinton is more intelligent than Trump and that she is better prepared to be president. But Clinton has lost her wide lead over Trump for having 'higher moral standards.' And Trump widens his lead over Clinton for being more honest and trustworthy."*

We are now in July, four months from the November election. By wide margins, the American people in these three swing states and in the entire country believe that "the old way of doing things no longer works and we need radical change."

Millions of Americans also believe that "trade agreements with other countries have hurt them and their families' financial situation."

These views are rock solid. They will not change in the next 4 months, no matter how many millions of dollars Hillary wastes on negative Trump ads.

Hillary represents the old way of doing things. Hillary represents the very unpopular NAFTA agreement which Bill pushed for and signed. Hillary was in favour of the Trans-Pacific Partnership Agreement before she was against it. Ha Ha!

Trump is the change candidate.

Hillary is the untrustworthy establishment candidate whom the American people believe is responsible for their worse financial situation.

Say good night, Hillary.

You are history.

July 15, 2016

Trump Taps Pence 4 VP - Go Hoosiers!

✶ ✶ ✶ ✶ ✶ ✶ ✶ ✶ ✶ ✶ ✶ ✶ ✶

Let me deal with the bad news first. Pretty minor after all. Though I do have some minor concerns that I will deal with at the latter part of this piece.

Previously, I had predicted that the Donald would select the Newt as his running mate. *Mea culpa*. My predictive powers failed me. So that is mostly bad news about me, not Trump. As I have previously written, some of this commentary is also about me.

But as one of the Donald's most important decisions as the GOP candidate, the Pence was very politically smart for several reasons.

Trump has a few political vulnerabilities. I know that may be a shock to true red Trump supporters. But Trump, for all his television exposure/experience (host of the very popular reality TV show *The Apprentice*,) his extensive social media ability, his command of the Twitterverse and of course his extensive private sector/ business acumen/ extensive real estate holdings, Trump lacks public sector and government experience.

Mike Pence goes a long way to fill those obvious gaps. Pence was a popular six term, twelve year veteran of Congress from Indiana. He is well liked by the socially conservative wing of the Republican Party and by Tea Party types, and is well respected by his Democratic colleagues across the aisle. He knows the ins and outs of lawmaking on the Hill. He knows how to sit down with both Democrats and GOP and get things done.

Pence also has some executive experience as he has been the governor of Indiana for the last three and half years.

Whereas the Donald could be a bit volatile, provocative and unpredictable in both word and deed, Pence is more reflective, calm, conservative and deliberative.

Pence is also a born-again Christian. A very religious man of integrity and moral character. A serious churchgoer. Married to the same woman for over thirty years. A man of strong family values. On the social conservative scale of values, Pence is considerably to the right of the more "New York values" Trump, in terms of same sex issues, pro-life versus pro-choice and Planned Parenthood.

Accordingly, Pence should firm up support on the Republican right and deter any Republican dissent by Trump haters and sore losers in the GOP camp (i.e. the Bushes and the Romneys.) Only 75 per cent of Republicans to date plan on voting for Trump. Pence should help the numbers increase to a more acceptable 90 per cent if not more.

There are millions of Evangelical Christians who normally are very active in the GOP election efforts, and who had been lukewarm to Trump's candidacy. Pence's selection has certainly excited the base, which is critical for the GOP and Trump's ground game and national election organizational efforts.

In addition, Pence and his conservative wing of the party are tied into some heavy hitting GOP donors like the famous Koch Brothers. Trump and his team will need some financial muscle in the home stretch to counter Hillary's shock and awe and massive negative media blitz closer to Election Day.

Though there may be some differences between Trump and Pence on the social conservative issues, they are on the same page as to Trump's analysis that the economy, previously mismanaged by both GOP and Democratic elites, has left many hardworking Americans behind financially. Note that in evangelical Indiana, Pence's own home state, Trump crushed Cruz, his staunch Christian opponent, because the people of Indiana preferred Trump's emphasis on the economy, and on the real loss of jobs and its devastating effects, rather than on refighting the abortion and transgender hot button issues.

It is critical for Trump and the GOP that the party be relatively unified and behind Trump's presidency in the upcoming GOP convention. I predict that the Pence factor and Trump's efforts in choosing Pence for the sake of party unity will go a long way to unifying the party.

My major caveat is that by choosing Pence, Trump passed up a chance to nominate a person less conservative than Pence and more attractive to the non-partisan independents who make up a significant faction in the country.

July 17, 2016

Trump Takes a Licking But Keeps on Kicking: The Second Coming of Donald J. Trump

✶ ✶ ✶ ✶ ✶ ✶ ✶ ✶ ✶ ✶ ✶ ✶ ✶

Recently I attended an informal urban summer party of political analysts and commentators of all political stripes, colors, shapes and sizes. What was cool about this venue was that the small urban townhouse had a unique backyard which ascended up to the mountain overlooking the city. The previous owner had built a series of ascending wooden decks, so this motley crew of iconoclastic pundits gathered high atop the city in a treehouse-like structure.

It was so jam. The evening had a certain unusual "boys only" vibe about it, though the presence of a single hard right feminist added a certain je ne sais quoi civilized and sophisticated quality to the evening.

The high point for me was the presence of our friend MJ, who is a brilliant political analyst of American politics, both past and present. The political genius of this dude is proved by the fact that he is reviled by both the left and the right. He revels in puncturing the myths and hypocrisies of both the left and the right.

MJ has an encyclopedic knowledge of Bill and Hillary Clinton, dating back to Bill's controversial time as Arkansas governor. And of course, he can cite sleazy chapter and verse about Bill's numerous bimbo eruptions both when he was Governor and President.

And of course, the varied and myriad Clinton scandals both past and of course present.

But what was particularly enlightening to me was MJ's hard-nosed analysis of Trump's chances in the Electoral College, from a clear-eyed state by state perspective.

MJ rationally concludes that the Trumpster will have a hard road to travel to successfully secure a majority in the Electoral College.

MJ pointed to some telling numbers that he had dug up.

For example, according to MJ:

"Utah, Georgia and Arizona (all states where Romney won by ten or more points) were far closer than they otherwise should be, all under six. Romney beat Obama in Utah by 48 points. Trump was tied with Clinton there."

"That means that Trump and the RNC are going to have to dump resources that neither has into these red states at the expense of the swing states. Every dollar that you spend defending Arizona is a dollar that can't be

spent winning Florida, Ohio and Pennsylvania, which are hugely expensive media markets."

MJ also suggested that Trump's demographic negatives were still toxic. According to MJ, Trump was still losing more than three out of four women, whereas Republicans usually win married women. "He's over 80 per cent negative with Hispanics, while the conventional wisdom is that they have to win about 40 per cent to win a general election. Finally, and worst of all, the Trump is now the first Republican since 1952 to be losing with college-educated whites."

But there is an old political rule in American politics:

"A week in politics is a lifetime. Three months is an eternity."

Since that party, over two weeks ago, several events occurred which accelerated the pro-Trump trends that I have been forecasting for months.

The head of the FBI, James Comey, nearly indicted Hillary Clinton for allegedly violating the Espionage Act for her "extremely careless ... negligent, almost but not quite grossly negligent" handling of secret and classified government documents through her unsecure BlackBerry. More specifically, through her unauthorized use of a private server/email system during her entire four-year term as Secretary of State, during which Hillary failed to officially disclose and that she or her lackeys lied about obtaining approval. As a result of this public shaming by the FBI chief, the majority of Americans believed her to be a lying piece of work, at least in this context.

Two black men were shot by white policemen. Both Obama and Hillary came down hard on the white cops and apparently blamed the entire criminal justice and law enforcement systems as being anti-black racists.

Then a black militant ex soldier killed five innocent policemen in broad daylight, citing Black Lives Matter and implicitly Obama and Hillary for supporting BLM's attack on all white cops as racist killers of black men.

Another radical Muslim terrorist, a Tunisian-born Muslim named Mohamed, killed over 80 innocent men, women and children in Nice by ramming a large truck through a crowd in Nice. ISIS claimed responsibility. Obama and Hillary refused to mention the R.M.T. words. Obama and Hillary apparently blamed the deaths on the work of a mentally unbalanced person and the lack of truck control. (The latter may not have happened but that is consistent with the Obama/Hillary narrative of blaming lone wolf mental illness and lack of gun control for clear radical Muslim terrorist activities.)

Republican presidential nominee Donald Trump nominated a very popular conservative Mike Pence, a former six-term, twelve-year veteran in Congress and current Governor of Indiana. This selection has helped Trump with his Republican base, firmed up support with the Republican caucus, dealt with his own personal lack of Washington public/political experience and has helped attract previously lukewarm Republican donors.

But now such changes to the political landscape have finally emerged in the harsh light of day. They are more out in the open. More visible and verifiable.

Accordingly, recent polls indicate that Trump is leading or has tied Hillary nationally, and has closed the gap against Hillary vis-a-vis women – Trump is only seven points down with women. Trump has secured 30 per cent of Hispanic vote and he is heading in the right direction, needing at least 40 per cent of the Hispanic vote to close the electoral deal. Trump has now secured majority support of white college-educated males.

In addition to these pro Trump events, what MJ does not appreciate is that we are in revolutionary times. The Obama/Hillary/liberal centre is not holding. The peasants (see worldwide) are revolting (see Brexit). And when I say peasants, I include angry men and women of all income levels, all educational levels, of all races, colors, creeds and ethnicities. From both the red states and the blue states and the inner cities where the elites play and work.

In other words, the silent majority, who are lying to all the pollsters and are supporting the Trumpster, but not revealing their true electoral choices until election day, are rising up. Yeats said it best:

THE SECOND COMING of Donald J. Trump (with further apologies to W.B. Yeats)

Turning and turning in the widening gyre
The falcon cannot hear the falconer;
Things fall apart; the centre (the Obama/Hillary coalition of climate change limousine liberals/social warrior extremists/white and black BLM supporters/radical Muslim terrorists deniers) cannot hold;
Mere anarchy is loosed upon the world,
The blood-dimmed tide is loosed, and everywhere
The ceremony of innocence is drowned;
The best lack all conviction, while the worst (see above liberal democrats)
Are full of passionate intensity.
Surely some revelation is at hand;
Surely the Second Coming is at hand.
The Second Coming! Hardly are those words out
When a vast image out of Spiritus Mundi
Troubles my sight: a waste of desert sand;
A shape with lion body (and the unique orange-shaded head of a 70-something New York billionaire/entrepreneur/ reality TV celebrity,)
A gaze blank and pitiless as the sun,
Is moving its slow thighs, (and large Gucci Loafer-covered feet) while all about it
Wind shadows of the indignant desert birds.
The darkness drops again but now I know
That twenty centuries of stony sleep
Were vexed to nightmare by a rocking cradle,
And what rough beast, its hour come round at last,
Slouches (wings in his Trump private jet) towards Bethlehem (Washington) to be born?

July 20, 2016

Hillary Chooses Her Soul Mate 4 VP-The Prince of Darkness (Satire)

★ ★ ★ ★ ★ ★ ★ ★ ★ ★ ★ ★ ★

In a move worthy of the scene-stealing Donald Trump, the Hillary has announced her choice for Vice President.

The Donald, his supporters and GOP officials are in an uproar as all the major American television networks have switched their coverage from the Republican National Convention to cover Hillary's controversial pick. Drum roll, please.

It's the *Prince of Darkness!*

No, it is not that nasty little Senator from Texas, Republican Ted Cruz, changing parties in revenge after being beaten and humiliated by the Trumpster.

Neither is it the other Prince of Darkness, Slick Willy "Bubba" Clinton, Hillary's "better half." Such a choice would be so wrong on so many different levels.

No, it is the real Prince of Darkness.

Lucifer. The Devil. Satan. Beezelbub

As Hillary explained in an exclusive interview to Wolf Blitzer on CNN:

Hillary: *"Wolf, as you know I am in the fight for my political life. Lucifer has been a close personal friend of mine and Bill's for many years. I have sought and followed his counsel often. We share the same lack of any morals and any shred of human decency. 'Luce,' as I like to refer to him, has been properly vetted. As suspected, he has slightly more skeletons in his large closet than I do, which should provide a distraction from me, for a change.*

"Also I need a down and dirty attack dog to take down that disgusting Trump, 'cause this is going to be a hell of a fight to the finish."

Wolf: *"Ms. Clinton, I know you are running as the climate change candidate. Your running mate, Mr. Lucifer, has publicly complained that in his home state in the deep, deep, deep south, Hades, it is not hot enough. He does not seem too fussed about all this climate change hoopla."*

Hillary: *"Oh Wolf, good one. Look a President/VP relationship is never perfect. My Bill was able to put up with that insufferable blowhard Al Gore for all those years. I'm sure 'Luce' and I could meet halfway. Wish me luck, Wolf. What do you think of our campaign slogan:"*

"The Clinton/Satan Ticket: Come Hell or Whitewater."

PART FOUR:

THE DEMOCRATIC AND GOP CONVENTIONS THE UFC OF POLITICAL SMACKDOWNS

LAME DUCK OBAMA/LYING HILLARY VS. CRAZY MAD DOG TRUMP

(**Writer's note:** *Until now, this collection of essays, comments and rants has followed an apparent chronological order. As the race heats up and events drive the narrative, for the sake of clarity, we will switch things up a bit.*

We will look at the Democratic convention first, especially Obama's and Hillary's speeches, and then look at the GOP convention and Trump's speech last.

But like everything about this crazy unconventional political year, expect some shocking revelations, political lives ruined, sleazy backroom plots and angry losers making public fools of themselves - and much, much more!!!)

July 21, 2016

Donald Trump May Have His Faults, But He Is No Racist

✶ ✶ ✶ ✶ ✶ ✶ ✶ ✶ ✶ ✶ ✶ ✶ ✶

To paraphrase Samuel Johnson, one of my favorite writers: "The accusation by liberals including Hillary Clinton that Donald Trump is a racist, is the last refuge of scoundrels."

Donald Trump was born in the 1940s and raised in the Borough of Queens, just outside Manhattan, the inner city of New York.

Trump has lived and worked practically all his life in New York as a developer, investor, owner and operator of apartments, hotels, condominiums and commercial properties.

New York is one of the most multicultural cities in the United States, with one of the largest nonwhite populations, containing very vibrant and large black and Hispanic communities as well as other major nonwhite immigrant groups.

I have been following and reading about the many exploits and business ventures of Donald Trump in New York and in adjoining New Jersey with respect to his casino ventures for over forty years. Throughout this time Trump and his myriad companies have employed thousands of people including many blacks and Hispanics.

At times Trump's practices may have been hard-nosed and tough, but to my knowledge Trump has never been criticized for being a bigot or racist in his personal life or business life in New York. And as a larger-than-life character in one of the biggest fishbowls in the world, Trump has been subject to *enormous* media scrutiny.

One of the most well-known and respected leaders of the black community in New York and by extension all of the United States is the Reverend Al Sharpton. Sharpton is a long time partisan Democrat, a close adviser to Barack Obama and a long time and loyal supporter of Hillary Clinton. Sharpton, a Brooklyn guy, has known Trump since the '70s.

Sharpton is a very successful New York and national power broker. He has hitched his star to Hillary. Hillary's success is his success. He has a lot to gain supporting Hillary and lots to lose if Trump wins the presidency and anoints other black men as the true representatives of black Americans in New York and country-wide.

So of course it's to Sharpton's interest to come down hard on Trump and in the process boost up Hillary's presidential chances with her and his black American base.

On the other hand, Trump, win or lose the presidency, will still be a powerful figure in New York, as will his children.

Trump and his family are true blue, street smart New Yorkers. Hillary is just a flyover New Yorker.

Sharpton does not want to frack with the Trumps on Trump's turf in New York.

Bottom line: In a major interview with Politico and in answer to the $64,000 Question - Is Trump a racist and bigot? - Sharpton's response was politically correct, very mild, even somewhat positive towards Trump, and as a result Sharpton's comments totally undermined Hillary's claim that Trump was a racist and a bigot.

Sharpton opined that he did not think Trump was a racist or bigot and he has known Trump since the '70s at least.

Sharpton conceded that he thought Trump's comments on Mexicans - as illegal migrants sneaking over the border and as rapists - and about temporarily banning Muslims from the US were bigoted, but then he characterized Trump (somewhat admiringly) as the white Don King.

Don King is a black fight promoter whom Trump befriended in the '80s to help Trump secure good fighters for his Atlantic City casinos.

In many ways Don King, Trump and Sharpton are all cut from the same street-hustling New York cloth. And I say that as a good thing.

At the Republican National Convention in Cleveland, Don King was in attendance in support of Donald Trump, and spoke very favorably of him. As did such other black notables as Dr. Ben Carson, who ran against Trump and ultimately dropped out and gave Trump his support.

And for the first time in decades, the GOP convention had many black speakers speaking in favor of Trump - with sincerity.

These black speakers were mainly black police chiefs, county commissioners or law and order sheriffs. Or black officers representing the American military.

They were not mere token speakers.

Their collective message spoke to the heart of Trump's campaign to make America Safe Again and Great Again.

Trump is very pro-military, pro-veteran, pro-law and order and pro-first responders, explicitly supporting police, firemen and emergency paramedics. He wholeheartedly praises the work these groups do. In New York and in the federal government, black men and women play significant roles therein and participate in large numbers.

Unbeknownst to the clueless liberal media, these public officials and members of the military, the police and other civil service organizations - hundreds of thousands, if not millions of men and women and their spouses, friends and children, many of whom are of color - are quietly and hugely supportive of Trump because he has supported them for years, both emotionally and financially. Basically he has their back. And they have his.

My point is that Hillary's attempt to dismiss Trump simply as a racist and a bigot has no basis in reality.

There is no evidence that Trump, throughout his personal and business life within New York and without, has engaged or acted in a racist and bigoted manner.

On the contrary, he enjoys enormous support from a large number of men and women from all walks of life in the New York black community and I suspect throughout the land.

Hillary's allegations rest solely on Trump's comments describing illegal Mexicans crossing the southern border as rapists. And his public desire to temporarily ban foreign Muslims from entering the United States.

Admittedly, Trump calling Mexican illegal aliens "rapists" was crude, rude and impolitic. I would like to believe that Trump was trying to distinguish himself at the time from the numerous better known politicians who had thrown their hats in the ring.

And that he was trying out some provocative ideas and themes, to gauge the public reaction. Both pro and con.

Interestingly, the response from the liberal media was swift and predictable as the media and the Democrats roundly condemned Trump for his incendiary use of language.

But such over the top language touched on a more universal truth. America was losing the ability to control its own borders and the safety of the American people was at risk. And the fault lay with the failure and weakness of the current Obama government and Hillary Clinton, who was a critical member of that government in the first term and was still closely aligned with her former boss.

The Republican Party to a man and woman stood for secure borders and increased security at the border.

But the problem for the majority of the Republicans was what to do with the 11 million illegal aliens currently residing in the United States. Obama wanted to grant millions of them the right to stay in the U.S.. The Republicans, as with many of Trump's opponents such as Marco Rubio and Jeb Bush, were caught trying to uphold the law, maintain secure borders, deal with the 11 million undocumented and try to attract Hispanic voters to the GOP cause.

As a result, these leading Republicans came across as conflicted, confused and impotent as Obama.

Whereas the first casualty of war is the truth, the first casualty of the American primaries is nuance.

I believe what the GOP base wanted instead of more Obama-like indecision, was simplicity, strength and certainty.

Hence Trump called out some of the illegal Mexican migrants as "rapists" and not Mexico's best, and then doubled down and insisted on building a wall to keep them out, adding that Mexico would pay for the wall.

"Build the Wall" became a simple but very effective rallying cry.

Similarly, Trump sensed that the American people were generally concerned that very bad people were in the United States and planning to commit terrorist acts in the name of Islam, as had been done on numerous occasions in various capitals of the world.

Once again Obama, his government and Hillary seemed incapable of coming to grips with this very real fear.

Yes, a majority of American Muslims were peace-loving, law-abiding citizens.

But all it took was a few bad actors to cause terrible damage in the US.

The Obama government seemed lost. They could not guarantee with certainty which Muslims from foreign lands or home-grown Muslims were radicalized and capable of committing horrible terrorist acts in the US.

The Obama government appeared to be sleep walking as potential radical Muslim terrorists were plotting within the US and the government did not have a clue as to who they were.

Hence Trump saw an opportunity to display tough and strong leadership, publicly arguing that since the government did not know who were the radicalized Islamic terrorists or potential terrorists among the American Muslim population, that no further Muslims should come from foreign lands into the U.S until the government got a better handle on the millions of Muslims in the U.S.

This time both the Democrats and the GOP were aghast at this seemingly biased and bigoted approach.

But Trump was right. The American people were frightened. They did not have confidence that the current government could protect them and hence this simple solution seemed the most effective and reasonable.

Subsequently Trump scaled back and insisted that there should be a temporary ban of certain people from certain troubled and dangerous foreign lands, but the principles held.

The bottom line was that the majority of Americans, both Democrats and Republicans, are more concerned about their safety and the safety of their families, about national security issues, and defending against radical Islamic terrorism, than political correctness.

I argue that the attempted public shaming of Trump and his supporters as racists and bigots has created a backlash against Hillary and her liberal supporters.

Poor Hillary and her liberal sycophants do not realize that the racist card has been overused and abused.

Hillary's use of the racist card has not stopped Trump or his supporters, but has in contrast emboldened them and made them stronger.

Frankly, without the power of the racist card and the sexist card, Hillary has very little to offer the American people.

I strongly believe that the tide has turned against her.

July 24, 2016

Hillary's DNC Sabotages Sanders Campaign

You can say and write all the bad things you want about the Republican convention and the GOP, but though the outsider Trump was not the GOP establishment's first choice (or the sixteenth choice for that matter) the GOP appeared to run a clean, fair, objective, impartial and democratic nomination/primaries process. Trump won fair and square.

According to the nearly 20,000 emails by DNC executives released by WikiLeaks, the DNC, under the authoritarian influence and control of Hillary and her sleazy minions, intentionally undermined and sabotaged the campaign of the insurgent Sanders and all the thousands of Sanders' supporters who spent months organizing and campaigning for Sanders. The same sleazy DNC executives also violated the trust of thousands and thousands of average Sanders donors who cumulatively contributed millions of dollars to his campaign.

There was no gross negligence here. All these acts were intentional, verging on criminality. The leaked emails are full of "smoking guns" which point the fingers at the Clinton/DNC executives who rigged the nomination in favor of Hillary.

Most notable was the DNC's efforts to cast aspersions on Sanders' religion. To question whether he was an observant Jew or not. The lowlife DNC types wanted to flush out info as to whether Sanders was a practicing Jew or an atheist.

In either case they were going to use his religion or non-belief in God against him in certain key religiously-oriented states. There is clear evidence that some DNC funds were used exclusively to help the Clinton campaign. Other emails demonstrated clear personal favoritism toward Hillary and disdain for Sanders, his supporters, and his campaign.

Other emails revealed dirty tricks that the DNC played on the Sanders team in order to suppress the vote for Sanders. The list of misdeeds goes on and on and on.

In response to the leaking of these damaging DNC emails, Sanders went on CNN and publicly stated that these emails are evidence of what Sanders and his team have been saying for months - that they believed the DNC was biased against him and his campaign. Accordingly, he called for the resignation of the DNC Chairman Debbie Wasserman Schultz.

If Democratic-friendly CNN is going hard and heavy on this Clinton scandal, then Hillary is in for a hell of a lot of pain this convention.

*(**NOTE:** As I write this, Wasserman Schultz has agreed to resign as the DNC chairman, though she will open and close the convention. Wasserman Schultz is just another one of many notable people whose reputations have been destroyed by their involvement with the toxic Clintons. Hillary threw Wasserman Schultz under Hillary's campaign bus. And ran her over a few times for good measure. The problem is that the whole executive of the much maligned DNC should resign. This was just another typical systematic corrupt Clinton operation very similar to Clinton's four year private email/server scandal. This was not careless or accidental but a planned and brutally executed sabotage of the Sanders campaign carried out daily and consistently practically from the time Sanders announced he had the guts to take on the venal and corrupt Hillary.)*

So will the Sanders delegates and supporters act like little wimps or will they rise up and protest the rigging of this nomination in favor of Hillary? Throwing Wasserman under the bus will not suffice. How about a do-over?

To add further insult to the already injured Sanders forces, at the same time of the WikiLeaks' disclosure, Michael Bloomberg - Mr. Wall Street; Mr. One Percent of the One Percent - announced that he was endorsing the lying, crooked Hillary. The clueless, arrogant, tone-deaf Bloomberg just added more gasoline to the grassroots working class/middle income fire spreading throughout the US, Europe and worldwide against the out-of-touch financial, political and socio-economic elites.

Hey Sanders rebels - how is that Sanders Revolution going? It seems the Clinton forces played you.

SUCKERS!!!

I love the smell of the well-oiled and corrupt Clinton political machine blowing up on national television!

Shame on Hillary, her people, the DNC and all those who support the most hated, venal and corrupt Democratic nominee to ever run for the American presidency.

It boggles the mind that apparently all Clinton supporters park their principles, their morals and their reason and utterly suspend disbelief when it comes to Hillary.

July 25, 2016

TacoGate: Hillary's DNC and its Racist Appeal to Hispanics

* * * * * * * * * * * * *

Ola! WikiLeaks strikes again. Hey, Latinos and Hispanics, how do you feel about being referred to by an arm of Hillary's campaign team, the Democratic National Committee, as "Taco Bowls"?

Clearly, you are nothing to Hillary and the Democrats but just mere votes to be used by her to secure power for herself and her friends.

I swear to the almighty Supreme Being, I could not make this horrible stuff up if I tried.

Amongst the nearly 20,000 emails of the DNC released by WikiLeaks, there was a devastating email from a Rebecca Christopher (Christopherr@dnc.org) - clearly a member of the DNC - in which she sent out an email entitled: "New video, Trump isn't trying to bring people together."

Apparently, Ms. Christopher sent out a script for a

proposed video to fellow DNC colleagues to vet and review.

This is what this disgusting and racist email* stated:

Date: Friday, May 6, 2016

Hi everyone,
Attached is a script for a new video we'd like to use to mop up some more taco bowl engagement, and demonstrate the Trump actually isn't trying.

Let me know if you have any flags and thank you!

Ms. Christopher, any flags? Are you fracking kidding me?

Referring to Hispanic Americans as "taco bowls" is so racist and demeaning. But so Hillary Clinton.

Hispanic Americans, black Americans, Muslim Americans - they're not real people to Hillary.

They are just voting blocs to the power-hungry Hillary to be used by her to grease her way to the American presidency.

I am so looking forward to DNC emails exposing Hillary's "chitlins and collard greens" outreach to black Americans.

And Hillary's "chopped liver and gefilte fish" defense of her Jewish American support.

*Check out this link for the actual email and the hysterical Twitter responses to this very revealing Hillary/DNC email and the attempt by Hillary supporters to blame the exposure of these emails on the Russians: **http://newsninja2012.com/dnc-email-leaks-show-racist-outreach-to-latinos-called-taco-bowl-engagement/**.

July 25, 2016

Democratic Convention: Day 1 - Prediction: Bernie's Bros Fighting Mad

* * * * * * * * * * * * *

Frankly, I was going to take a pass on this Democratic convention as I thought that this would be a heavily-scripted, boring four-day Hillary Clinton love-in. But then the WikiLeaks dump of 20,000 emails of Democratic National Committee staffers occurred, exposing for all to see the premeditated, planned, consistent destruction by DNC staffers (all loyal to Hillary) of the Sanders' campaign in opposition to Hillary.

The Sanders delegates are angry and rightfully so.

I predict that this convention will go far worse than Hillary and her lackeys ever imagined.

Here is why.

The internal emails showed a consistent pattern of pro-Hillary and anti-Sanders behavior not only by the recently departed chair of DNC Debbie Wasserman Schultz, but by all major DNC staffers and by many DNC executives, including Donna Brazile, vice chair of the DNC, now promoted to chair to replace the departed Wasserman Schultz.

Ironically, there are emails of Brazile dissing and badmouthing Sanders and the Sanders campaign for complaining about the undemocratic involvement of so many super delegates already in the pocket of Hillary, even before the primaries started. So I do not think the ascension of Brazile to the chair will pacify the Sanders forces.

*(**TRIGGER WARNING:** Beware the following snide aside about Hillary always trotting out black American spokesmen to counter criticism of her. In other words, trying to provide a positive spin to a Hillary lie, misdeed or scandal. Otherwise known as "Affirmative Reaction.")*

Yesterday, a black female spokesman for Hillary and the DNC was interviewed live on *CNN* responding to the controversial emails. This woman first said she had not read these emails. So she could not comment on them.

Then she questioned the validity and truthfulness of these apparent accurate emails sent between DNC staffers.

Then she defended Hillary by stating that these emails are irrelevant just like the thousands of emails investigated by the FBI relating to Hillary's unauthorized use of personal email and a private server.

In other words, her response was totally nonsensical, evasive, inarticulate and downright stupid.

Now if an old angry Democratic white guy had come out with these stupid useless comments, the press and the public would be all over what an incompetent loser this jerk was.

But because these same illogical words were uttered by a black woman, for some reason, she is immune from criticism because to criticize a black spokesperson would be considered "racist" in polite politically correct company.

As we have seen from the now-discredited and disastrous Black Lives Matter publicity debacle, liberal Democrats and the liberal press have gone to this poor disadvantaged and discriminated well once too often.

A backlash - or blacklash - has occurred with counter slogans as "Blue Lives Matter," "All Lives Matter," and more recently "All Americans Matter."

So I predict that even longtime Democratic official and commentator Donna Brazile spinning and defending the indefensible Hillary will not be immune from the wrath of the Sanders forces and of course the vilification of the American people, regardless of political stripe.

The revolution may have been started by and originally led by Bernie Sanders, but once he officially lost, then formally endorsed and supported Hillary Clinton as the

Democratic presidential nominee, I believe that he has lost control of his forces. I believe that this revolution in the Democratic ranks will continue, notwithstanding Sanders' formal endorsement of Hillary on Monday night at the convention. Because a revolt against the Democratic elites and the political establishment has gone rogue and has taken on a life of itself.

The Sanders forces are not just angry with Wasserman Schultz and the DNC; they are also livid about Hillary's apparent betrayal and her apparent manipulation of the DNC to sabotage the Sanders campaign.

Over the week-end Sanders forces publicly protested in Philadelphia and as reported in the Wall Street Journal, the Sanders forces were heard to chant the popular anti- Hillary Republican refrain, "Lock her up."

Notwithstanding that Sanders had called for Wasserman Schultz's resignation and that she had complied over the weekend, the Sanders forces still showed up at a Florida delegation morning breakfast on Monday and lustily booed Wasserman. Which of course was videoed and immediately uploaded online for millions to see.

It was pretty amazing seeing Democratic delegates booing and holding up signs stating "Emails" at this breakfast meeting. These Sanders people are royally upset and they want to voice their disgust loudly and clearly. In a speech before the convention, Sanders endorsed Hillary, but then he was booed by his supporters. More evidence that the protest will continue, with or without Bernie. I suspect Bernie bros feel #BernedbyBern.

Other reasons the Sanders forces will make a scene is that these forces do not trust Hillary. They believe her to be a liar and a criminal, who at least should have been indicted for allegedly violating the Espionage Act, by apparently acting in a gross negligent manner in coming into possession of documents related to national defense outside of proper government secure and custodial control.

The Sanders forces view the selection of Tim Kaine, Hillary's vice president nominee - an apologist for Wall Street banks and the oil and gas industry - as a huge slap in the face to the allegedly revolutionary and progressive movement in the Democratic Party started by Sanders.

This will now be a very exciting convention. I predict the well-organized and very angry Sanders forces will not play ball with the Clinton forces who want to project an image of unity to the American public.

I believe that some of the Sanders people will put principle over expediency and not cave to Clinton.

Time will tell.

July 26, 2016

Democratic Convention: Day 1 - Sanders Delegates Trash Hillary Love Fest

* * * * * * * * * * * * *

Over the weekend, just prior to the first day of the Democratic convention, WikiLeaks released damning emails by DNC officials which showed that allegedly the impartial Democratic National Committee was really an arm of the thoroughly immoral Clinton campaign, and that the DNC officials systematically sabotaged and/or undermined the Sanders campaign, from Debbie Wasserman Schultz, the chair, to Donna Brazile, the vice chair, through to the majority if not all the DNC staffers.

Once the nearly 20,000 DNC emails were released, Sanders forces went absolutely and rightfully batshite crazy. I kid you not, the Wall Street Journal reported Sanders protesters demonstrating on the streets of Philadelphia outside the hall, chanting "lock her up, lock her up."

This was not exactly how the Hillary forces wanted to present the new, improved, cleaner and more trustworthy Hillary Clinton to the national television audience.

Wasserman Schultz agreed to resign after the convention.

However, her resignation did not placate upset and angry Sanders forces.

Sanders' well-organized delegates attended a Monday morning breakfast meeting of Wasserman Schultz's Florida delegation and they lustily booed Wasserman while she was speaking.

This was of course captured on YouTube and spread to millions of happy Trump supporters.

Then the Hillary forces and Hillary-controlled DNC went into full-on damage control.

They urged Sanders to gain control of his angry delegates who had gone off message - big time.

So much for love and unity on day one of this convention.

It seems Sanders was ordered to speak to a crowd of Sanders delegates in the afternoon prior to the official opening of the convention.

Sanders outlined the meagre achievements of the Sanders revolution to a crowd of supporters. He boasted that the Sanders forces had secured five meaningless committee chair positions. Big Whoop. Sanders then exclaimed that the revolution would continue and he urged his supporters to vote for Hillary.

Sanders' public plea to vote for Hillary was met with boos.

Clearly, the old man had lost it. He had lost the crowd. He had lost their respect.

Many of the Sanders delegates had now gone rogue.

He had sold out - but for what?

A so-called meaningless progressive platform that Hillary will trash in August once the campaign has been fully launched for the race to the presidency.

WikiLeaks also revealed very close relationships between major reporters in all news organizations such as NBC, CNN, the *New York Times, Washington Post* and Politico, implying they are all biased and in the pocket of Hillary.

Surprise, surprise, surprise.

So the first night of primetime, the convention is called to order.

Wasserman Schultz as chair was supposed to still open and close the convention.

She was urged not to attend for fear that she would be

booed down by Sanders delegates who were still rightfully upset, and were no longer following Sanders' orders to desist from protesting in favor of Sanders during the first night of the convention.

Donna Brazile, the vice chair, was supposed to take Wasserman's place at the podium but she was also outed as an anti-Sanders, pro-Hillary operative within the DNC whose emails indicated she hated Sanders and was willing to "cuss" him and his organization.

So Donna Brazile was a no show as well.

To add further insult to injury, Wasserman was reported to have resigned as the chair of DNC, but then was immediately hired by Hillary Clinton for her presidential campaign.

Once again proving that Hillary has loyalty to her people who do dirty tricks for her.

The Clintons have been doing these types of dirty tricks for years and they keep getting away with it with the liberal mainstream press.

Back at the convention, some black female minister was giving the invocation and when she urged everyone to get behind Hillary and vote for her, the Sanders people booed the black female minister. On prime time television!

That was so precious.

The high point for me was when comedienne Sarah Silverman, a Bernie supporter, spoke in favor of Hillary Clinton and was booed by the Sanders people. So she turned around and told the "Bernie or bust" people that they were "ridiculous."

That arrogant and insensitive comment further incited the crowd to boo her and Hillary more.

Now that was great television!

We learned on the floor that many Sanders delegates believed that Sanders had caved and given up much too soon.

They wanted a debate on the floor about TPP, the Trans-Pacific Partnership Trade Agreement which the Sanders people strongly oppose.

The Sanders people wanted also to debate the future role of super delegates in subsequent primary contests.

Both of these matters were prevented from going to the floor.

At the end of the night Sanders did give his traditional primary stump speech and at the end he heartily endorsed Hillary.

But clearly the revolution and his people had moved on from Sanders.

Many Sanders people interviewed that night refused to work for or vote for Hillary.

The first night was a disaster for the Hillary forces.

Best laid plans of rats and morally-compromised Hillary women.

July 27, 2016

Hillary Love Fest - Day 2 - Slick Willy's Creepy Tale of Stalking Hillary

A good friend of mine - a Clinton supporter and an educated man with a university degree or two - was very impressed with Hillary after listening to Bill babble on for over fifty minutes about their wonderful, very loving life together based on trust, faithfulness and mutual respect.

Of course I had a slightly different take on the speech.

I liked MSNBC commentator Rachel Maddow's comments. (Rachel, a dyed in the wool liberal feminist, is no friend of Trump.)

She found Bill Clinton's first part of the speech really creepy and off-message.

Bill spent the first ten to fifteen minutes talking about how he stalked Hillary for a date, even lying to her face while standing in line to register for law school classes when he had previously registered. Pure Slick Willy.

Then how he kept on wanting to marry her and he kept on proposing and she kept on rejecting him.

I kept thinking: Hillary, get out. Get out now. Because if you don't, you will face a life of shame and grief and hurt because of this disgusting philandering horn dog, who has no respect for you as a woman, as a person and as a future partner.

Bill then talked about loving to walk and talk with Hillary as they were dating. Little did she know that he would be stepping out on her - multiple times the rest of her sorry life, with multiple partners.

I love the way the Clintons rewrite history. On PBS David Brooks and Mark Shields - no friends of Trump - could not help but remark that Hillary's health care plan in the '90s was a complete disaster. How she was so secretive and how her plan was too complicated and how she alienated both the Democrats and GOP in both houses with a politically tone-deaf plan that led to Slick Willy losing both houses after his first term.

Secretive, bad policy, bad judgment and bad political instincts. These are the traits of Hillary. Hillary and the liberals and the Democrats think the American people are all uneducated white trash who can't read and can't remember all the horrible things she has done over twenty-five years of scandals.

What about all those bimbo eruptions, Bill, when you

were Governor in Arkansas and then in the White House? What about Monica, the blue dress, and you being impeached?

In fifty minutes of blabbing we did not hear all that other stuff about this wonderful, loving, faithful relationship.

We also did not hear anything about Bill's wonderful work at the Clinton Foundation, where Bill raised hundreds of millions of dollars from foreign countries and multinational companies that allegedly did business with the American government and the State Department, led coincidentally by Hillary Clinton.

I would have loved to hear Slick Willy dance around the allegation that he and his wife were allegedly engaged in some multimillion dollar pay-for-play government deals.

"I want you to listen to me. The Clinton Foundation and I did not have financial relations with that woman, Mrs. Clinton."

The real story was that a large number of Sanders' delegates had left the hall in disgust, vowing to vote for the Green party, or not vote for any one - or even to vote for Trump.

If Trump had been running against Bernie, do you actually think that he would have bought off the whole DNC to rig the election against Bernie, like Hillary did? And then have the chutzpah to hire Wasserman Schultz for his own campaign as pay back for all of Wasserman Schultz's dirty tricks against Bernie?

Only Hillary would stoop so low and be so blatantly evil. Knowing that the supine liberal mainstream press would once again, as they have done for the Clintons all these past twenty-five years, give them a pass.

Hey, but Hillary - she's great with the kids! Remember - she will be a great role model for young women on how to lie, cheat, look the other way with philandering partners and buy loyalty and rig elections.

July 27, 2016

Barack's Convention Speech - Icarus Obama Flies Too Close to the Sun - Finally Crashes and Burns

* * * * * * * * * * * * *

(NOTE: For a change of pace and structure, I have chosen thematic structure over simple chronology. In other words, instead of reviewing the Trump speech, I have jumped ahead to the Obama speech and then I will double back to both Trump's and Hillary's speeches and their visions of America past, present and future.

In reviewing the arc of this story, it has become very apparent that this election has become two competing visions of the policies and programs of the Obama administration these past eight years. Hence to better understand and comment on the Trump visions/programs versus the Hillary visions/ programs, I want to focus first at length on the Obama administration.)

As predicted, on the third night of the Democratic Convention Barack Hussein Obama II gave the worst speech of his career as he tried to defend his pitiful and meagre legislative record, his extremely disappointing Administration and the indefensible and nearly indictable Hillary.

But this should not come as any surprise to us pundits and analysts who have had to sit through for the last eight years and listen to Obama's boring, self-indulgent and self-regarding personal stories, year in and year out.

Obama's personal story was interesting the first time. But again and again, when he had nothing better to say, Obama would return and draw upon the same lame story.

You were born to a white Kansas woman and black Kenyan father who abandoned you at an early age. You were raised by your white Kansan, salt of the earth, grandparents. You learned strong American values from them. But you felt incomplete. You did not know who you really are. You needed to search for your true black African identity and in the process find out the truth about your father and yourself. We get it. You have daddy issues.

The lives of young black men abandoned by their black fathers matter.

Somehow your story is the story of America searching for its roots, its identity. Its soul.

Or the solution to many of the ills of urban black society.

But come on, Barack, get over yourself. You have a country to run, man.

Excuse me. I digress.

When Obama burst into the public consciousness he was, admittedly, a novelty.

The year was 2007. Obama was contesting against then-Senator Biden for the Democratic nomination for president.

I can still hear old Joe Biden refer to the junior senator from Illinois as follows:

"I mean, you got the first mainstream African-American who is articulate and bright and clean and a nice-looking guy," Biden said. "I mean, that's a storybook, man."

Now if a Republican had made these same comments, he would have been publicly shamed and rode out of town on a rail as a racist by the liberal mainstream press.

I think old Joe was referring to some other black leaders, like the Reverend Jesse Jackson, who seemed more militant, angrier, a little rough around the edges and not as slim, fit and nicely attired as Obama.

In other words Jackson was too scary as a black man to be a future American leader - and clearly not as palatable and presentable to the greater white American electorate as the half-white, half-black and just-right Obama.

Yes, Obama at that time was mainstream African-American, articulate, bright, clean and nice-looking. And that was definitely storybook, man.

But as I will point out, by the end of Obama's eight year run he was still articulate in a very superficial way, but he was definitely not as bright and he was not as clean.

Obama, in the early years, spoke beautifully. His speeches soared and inspired. Especially when he spoke about his own interesting story - the product of a white American woman and a Kenyan black man who abandoned him at an early age, and his search for his black identity and his Kenyan roots.

You see in the early years Obama was always at his best when he talked about his own story. And then he was able to masterfully weave his personal story of being half-white and half-Kenyan into the greater story of America.

At the 2004 Democratic National Convention Obama said that he believed there was neither a liberal America nor a conservative America, but a United States of America. Obama also stated that there was not a black America, a white America, a Latino America or an Asian America, but the United States of America.

Obama also talked critically about red states (Republican) and blue states (Democratic.)

In winning the 2008 Presidential election, Obama talked about hope and change until the cows came home.

You see, Obama could eloquently talk and talk about his vision of a color blind America and the need to unify the country.

He just had no plan. And with no plan, he had no idea how to realize his lofty visions.

That is Obama's presidency in a nutshell.

Fast forward to 2016.

Obama's Defense of His Presidency

On Wednesday night at the Democratic Convention Obama tried to eloquently and persuasively defend his eight years in office. He failed miserably.

Where in 2008, a self-confident and self-assured Obama reached for the stars, eight years later a clearly small and diminished Obama relied on meaningless banalities.

Obama prattled on, bathetically. He said, basically, that America is still great.

In fact, America is better than great.

The streets are safe. Business is fine. Jobs are being created. Michelle and I are doing fine.

So are our beautiful daughters being educated at fancy private schools.

Osama bin laden was killed by me personally, as if I crushed out his life with my bare hands.

Basically, everything is pretty hunky dory. Joe Biden and I did a great job.

Mission accomplished.

Yah, we have some issues. We have some economic problems. Some people have been left by the wayside. But we are strong and we are stronger together.

And I am supporting Hillary Clinton because if that other fellow wins, my only legacy, the much maligned and flawed Obamacare, will be taken off life support.

Hey Obama, how is that hopey and changey theme coming along?

The fact is that after eight years of flowery, soaring, inspirational quoting the Declaration of Independence and name-dropping Lincoln, Obama has been publicly exposed to be "all hat and no cattle."

There was no substance to his words. There was no follow up legislative plan of action. There are never ever any concrete legislative and policy achievements.

Obama came to power in 2008 with Democratic majorities in both the Senate and the House of Representatives. By 2012, Obama and the Democrats had been reduced to minority status in both Houses. Obama was largely responsible for that political debacle.

I recall how Rahm Emanuel, Obama's chief of staff - point man with Nancy Pelosi to ram through Obamacare - warned Obama that by proceeding with Obamacare, the Democrats would lose control of both Houses by the 2012 election. Typically Obama ignored his advice. Emanuel was right. Obama - horribly wrong.

Obama won the battle for Obamacare, but he lost the war with the Republicans for the remainder of his Administration.

Obama won the presidency in 2012, but his legislative record was non-existent in the second term.

Obama was reduced to pathetically struggling to make policy through constitutionally questionable and democratically questionable presidential executive orders. Do you remember Obama's attempt to grant permanent status to 5 million illegal immigrants with a wave of his wand. Shot down by the Supreme Court as being grossly unconstitutional.

Hey, you clueless, hypocritical liberals, shame on you! Your own guy, in his second term, became the real dictatorial strong man as he treated America like his own private banana republic while you liberals stood silent, out of political correctness. How about when he interfered in an ongoing FBI Investigation of Hillary and her private email/server taking national defense documents out of secure government custody? And do you think Attorney General Loretta Lynch, during the same FBI investigation, met secretly with Bill Clinton on the famous tarmac without Obama's knowledge?

Was it liberal guilt that prevented you from publicly criticizing your very flawed and dangerous black President?

Hey, in my exuberance and disgust of Obama, I am getting a little ahead of myself.

I apologize.

Obama's Minimal Domestic Accomplishments

In his first four years, Obama's singular and only noteworthy piece of legislation was the heavily flawed Obamacare.

Obama manipulated the passage of this legislation by going on national television and lying to the American people.

Remember how he spoke with forked tongue, "If you like your doctor, you can keep your doctor…If you like your health plan, you'll be able to keep your health plan."

Lies, lies, and more lies.

Hey, Obama, you are no longer fabulous. You are a fabulist, a mythomaniac, a prevaricator, a perjurer.

As to keeping your own doctor,

NO, YOU CAN'T!!!

Even, the liberal architect of Obamacare admitted publicly that Obama and his administration had misled the American people in order to obtain public approval and support. He boasted how he and the Obama team had put one over the ignorant American populace. He was positively Obamaesque in his condescending and superior attitude to the people he was supposed to help and serve.

And that was Obama's key legislative achievement for his entire eight years.

New York Times columnist Maureen Dowd attributed Obama's ineffectiveness as a legislator to Obama's own character and personality.

Dowd continuously criticized Obama for being a terribly aloof and disengaged president when it came to the nuts and bolts and nitty gritty of developing and getting passed key legislation through both Houses.

Basically, Obama had no interest in securing the support of his own Democrats on the Hill. He never picked up the phone to call and to schmooze with Democrats in his own party, let alone the opposition.

Obama was just not a backslapping, deal-making politician - to his discredit.

Obama had no interest in bargaining and negotiating with Congress. It was beneath him.

He was the vision guy. The hopey and changey guy.

His strange Obama-like view of government was that all he had to do was orate like Cicero and legislation would magically get passed.

How did that work out for you, Barry?

Well, it did not work out very well. Even for Obama's signature Obamacare. I always thought that it was very strange, with respect to so important a piece of legislation, that Obama had let then-House Majority leader Nancy Pelosi carry the can on that legislation.

Here was the first sign of what would become classic Obama, doing his pathetic and infamous "leading from behind" schtick.

In other words - a spineless, disengaged, disinterested approach to leading a country. Hiding behind a woman's skirt. Actually a whole coterie of womens' skirts: Michelle, Valerie Jarrett, Susan Rice and Hillary Clinton. We knew who wore the pant suit in that Administration.

Essentially, Obama was regularly "pussy-whipped" into action by this very strong group of women with whom he surrounded himself for support.

To prop him up - to give him backbone.

This type of governing might work on Oprah or The View but for the leader of the most powerful country of the world - to the predominantly strong men leaders in the rest of the world, the leaders of China and Russia, in Europe, the Middle East, Japan and India - not so much.

I predict Obama's presidency will go down in history as the "Pussy-Whipped Presidency".

In order to successfully deal and navigate this complex legislation through Congress, Obama had to be on his game. Instead, when the chips were down, Obama was hardly in the room. He was non-existent. He had no game.

Obama demonstrated that he had neither the interest, the patience nor the ability to work in the trenches with Congress to push through the Obamacare deal. This disinterest, this detachment and inability to lead legislatively, became a pattern of behavior that Obama repeated over and over again throughout his failed and mediocre administration.

The Economy - Obama Played Golf and Kowtowed to Wall Street While Blue Collar and Middle Income Jobs Were Lost

During Obama's Administration, the Economist has estimated that about five to eight million good paying manufacturing jobs were lost as a result of America's overly generous and unfair free trade agreements. These jobs were never replaced. In addition, millions of Americans with blue collar or middle income jobs had their salaries effectively frozen during this period. Despite government promises, these workers were never properly compensated or retrained to replace their well-paid manufacturing jobs.

It is no wonder that millions of Americans have rebelled against Obama, and the elites of both parties, for their ignoring the plight of these workers, mostly centered in the American heartland of Wisconsin, Iowa, Ohio, Michigan, Illinois, Minnesota, North and South Dakota, Kansas, Missouri and Nebraska – and in many pockets of the United States where blue collar and middle income jobs were lost to foreign competitors and the outsourcing of these jobs by American multinationals.

Obama expended most of his limited energy and focus on passing the flawed Obamacare legislation and bailing out Wall Street banks and bankers, while ignoring the plight of millions of average working families.

Illegal Immigration

Illegal immigration is a far greater problem for average and lower income Americans than has been disclosed by the Obama government.

There are approximately over 11 million illegal immigrants in the U. S., mostly coming from Mexico and South and Central America. There are huge costs for the border states to bear in terms of providing health and educational services, together with administration, border control and enforcement for these 11 million illegal immigrants.

Furthermore, the influx of such workers diminish the wages of American citizens at the lower end of the scale, affecting mostly black and Hispanic Americans.

Climate Change Policies – A Non-Starter

In previous speeches, Obama had spoken eloquently about the ills of climate change and the need to protect the earth and the environment for future generations of Americans.

The reality is that Obama was a total failure in translating his soaring rhetoric on the adverse consequences of climate change into serious, comprehensive policies. Consequently, his climate change policies are a non-starter and dead in the water. Obama had eight years to do something with

Congress. He failed miserably.

For Obama, climate change policies and solutions were also to be part of his legacy, but he failed to mention much about climate change in his rambling over-long speech on Wednesday.

Safety and Security at Home

Though Obama talked a great game in 2008 about being a post racial president and bringing America together, in 2016, America is worse than it was in 2008.

America is more divided along racial lines than ever.

In the last year, unfortunately, some black men have been killed by white police officers.

Just as tragically, as a result of Obama's lack of leadership, his bias toward Black Lives Matters thugs and his indifference to the lives of police who protect American citizens, during the last years of his administration there has been a significant rise of police officers being ambushed and killed by black American snipers.

For example, just recently a black ex military sniper killed five Dallas cops and injured seven.

Another black ex-military man killed three Baton Rouge policemen and wounded three other cops.

Both of these incidents of killings were in retaliation.

These tragic events have pitted black anti-cop citizens against white pro-law and order and pro-cop citizens.

Obama did not help matters when subsequent to the black men being killed in Minnesota and Louisiana, he appeared to favor the anti-cop position of Black Lives Matter (BLM) over the lives of policemen who put their lives on the line every day to protect American residents.

In addition, during the Obama administration, black-on-black killings in such heavily black cities as Chicago, Detroit and Baltimore rose at alarming rates. A little known fact: For every black man killed by a white cop, there are 40 killings of black men by other black men.

The blame for the rising number of homicides in black urban communities should also be put firmly on Obama's shoulders and on both of his second-rate Attorneys General Holder and Lynch. Out of political correctness Obama and his chief legal enforcement officers placed undue restrictions on local police. Consequently these very same police have not been able to properly do their jobs to protect the communities.

The result: The bad actors have flourished.

And all American citizens, regardless of color, in these dangerous urban areas, have been at risk due to Obama's negligence and poor judgment.

Crime and law and order are back on the public agenda. American people, regardless of race, color and ethnicity are concerned about the safety of their streets and communities. But according to Obama, everything is fine.

National Security

On Obama's watch, the following major radical Islamic terrorist attacks have been launched against the American people coming from within America's borders.

On November 4, 2009, at Fort Hood, Texas, a Muslim doctor killed thirteen unarmed soldiers and injured thirty-one while praising Allah.

On September 11, 2011, in Waltham, Massachusetts, Muslim terrorists slashed the throats of three Jewish men.

On February 7, 2013, in Buena Vista, New Jersey, a radical Muslim targeted and beheaded two Coptic Christians.

On April 13, 2013, in Boston, Massachusetts, two foreign-born Muslims who self-identified as being very religious detonated two horrible bombs containing ball bearings at the finish line of the Boston Marathon. They killed three people and several others lost their limbs. Over 264 innocent people were injured.

On July 16, 2015, in Chattanooga, Tennessee, another radical religious Muslim terrorist engaged in a suicide mission at a recruiting centre and naval centre in a mall which left five dead.

On December 2, 2015, in San Bernardino, California, a husband and wife team of radical Islamic terrorists killed fourteen people at a Christmas party.

On June 13, 2016, in Orlando, Florida, another radical Islamic terrorist went into a gay bar, massacred forty-nine people and wounded fifty-three other innocent people.

For eight years now, Obama's response to these very clear and dangerous acts of radical Islamic terrorists has been odd and very disturbing.

In just about all the cases, there was very clear and concrete evidence that these perpetuators were Muslims and they were acting in the service of Islam, Allah, ISIS, ISIS clones, specific ISIS leaders or other radical Islamic terrorist leaders. Oftentimes these terrorists would post to Facebook prior, during or post-terrorist act, claiming allegiance to any of the above. They would call up 911 prior to these horrible events. They would communicate their loyalty to ISIS and the Islamic cause with police authorities during or after these horrific events. These crazy murderous lunatic Islamic murderers would yell their hateful messages from the highest mosque or go on CNN or Fox and visibly and publicly proclaim their loyalty to ISIS if given half a chance.

There has never been an effort by these radical Islamic terrorists to hide their motives or the reasons for massacring innocent American men, women and children.

Despite all this evidence that these were without any question or qualification acts by radical Islamic terrorists, for the last eight years Obama and his officials have refused to identify them as such.

Say what?

At various times Obama took to calling them, "mentally unbalanced," "lone wolves," "home-grown radicals" or "confused young men."

At other times Obama and his officials would try to hide the names or religion of these terrorists and instead try to distract the American public by blaming lack of gun control as the cause of these terrorist acts.

After being continuously criticized, reviled and mocked by his critics for stubbornly refusing to say the three magical words - "radical Islamic terrorists" - Obama starting using his characteristic legal sleight of hand language. Sophistry, that is - the use of fallacious arguments with the intention of deception.

You see, I do not think Obama is an ignorant man. Certainly, he does not have the first rate mind, he thinks he possesses.

His is a second-rate mind. And a dangerous one at that. You know the expression "a little knowledge is a dangerous thing"? I have come to believe that Obama is a very dangerous man.

He is clever, in an evil way. But not so intelligent or clever to be successfully deceptive and devious.

That takes real intelligence, which clearly Obama is lacking.

If you look at him critically, in a cold-eyed manner, shorn of liberal guilt over his race and color, Obama is transparently mendacious and deceptive - hence, evil.

Obama and his fellow elitist liberals think that he is superior to his fellow Americans. In fact he and those liberal officials think that the American people are quite stupid or so wrapped up in their own affairs that they can be swayed with fine-sounding words and complex concepts, as with Obamacare.

As previously noted, Obama and his people crafted Obamacare with such complexity that they believed they would be able to fool people into supporting something that was beyond their comprehension and knowledge.

Obama and his people succeeded with this strategy, so they tried this same convoluted and deceptive public strategy in order to downplay the real and present threat to Americans of radical Islamic terrorism.

Unfortunately for Obama, but fortunately for America, Obama failed miserably.

Let me explain.

Obama and his people are the masters of spin. Of disinformation and distraction.

And of the Big Lie.

The thinking is that if Obama and his spinmeisters keep telling The Big Lie, over and over again, in such presentable and logical ways, then it becomes accepted wisdom, The truth.

One of Obama's Big Lies is that America cannot identify the murderous thugs as "radical Islamic terrorists" because that would be against America's national security interests. This dangerous logic is as follows:

America needs its Muslim allies in the Middle East on the ground to fight ISIS, or as Obama calls them, the more user-friendly "ISIL" or "Daesh.".

So if Americans refer to murderous thugs who shoot, blow up, behead and injure innocent Americans using those three bad words (radical Islamic terrorists) it will alienate our moderate Middle Eastern Muslim allies who are fighting ISIS on the ground on behalf of Americans.

Alternatively, the use of those three bad words could inflame moderate Muslims in the Middle East and in the U.S. and turn them into those three bad words we can't mention.

Alternatively, if you refer to these people as "radical Islamic terrorists," who claim to be acting on behalf of ISIS, you are just empowering and emboldening these people. The magical stupid thinking is that if the American government does not mention ISIS by name in connection with these horrible massacres, somehow America will win the propaganda war.

Except, you brainless, elitist, liberal nincompoops, America no longer controls the means of information.

Hello, there is something new around called the internet. The world does not rely on CBS, NBC, ABC, CNN (aka the Clinton News Network), the *New York Times* or the *Washington Post* for its news. (If it ever did.)

Because forty-nine people are killed by an ISIS-inspired radical Islamic terrorist and it is not initially reported by the Obama-controlled liberal mainstream press, this event did not happen?

ISIS was not involved in this travesty and tragedy?

To any intelligent person with common sense - and we are not talking the overly educated Washington elite - this is all spin, deception, disinformation.

Blah, Blah, Blah and more Blah.

Frankly, I can't buy this BS. And clearly neither do the American people and the rest of the world, who obtain their information from other sources. How about from ISIS directly?

Could you imagine Churchill or FDR during World War II refusing to call Hitler and his murderous followers Nazis for fear of alienating the good and peace-loving Germans in Germany, or for fear of Germanophobia in the United States against German-born American citizens or residents?

Decent leaders have the courage to call out evil when they see it.

They have the knowledge, experience and judgment to face evil, accurately identify it and then fight to destroy it for good.

But if you cannot identify the enemy or you are unwilling and incapable of identifying the enemy, then how can you have the will and the determination to defeat the enemy?

Clearly, Obama cannot identify the enemy, and he does not have the will or determination to defeat the enemy for good.

Another Big Lie of Obama is that "Islam is a religion of peace." Obama's corollary argument is that those mentally unbalanced persons in America who have killed Americans, citing ISIS, and following Allah, are not real Muslims, but just sick people who are following an extremist ideology.

Obama's second corollary argument is that if you identify these terrorists as Islamic terrorists, then all Muslims in America will be tarred with the same terrorist brush and will be victims of Islamophobia, unfairly and unjustly. So for the sake of protecting the feelings of American Muslims, for Obama, it is preferable to deceive the American people.

Newt Gingrich in his speech during the Republican Convention provided the best counter arguments to Obama's Big Lies when he stated that the majority of Muslims in the world and in the US are peace-loving people.

But numerous surveys have indicated that 10 per cent to 25 per cent of Muslims are sympathetic to the radical Islamic terrorist goals and actions of ISIS.

In America where there are about three million Muslims, at minimum 300,000 Muslims may be radical or subject to radicalism. As a result, there are elements within the Muslim community that are violent or may be violent and America must be vigilant in order to protect Americans from more violent terrorist attacks within its borders by its own Muslim Americans.

I do not know with certainty why Obama refuses to admit that there is a serious radical Islamic terrorist threat within the United States.

For public and political purposes Obama says that he is Christian. But based on a close reading of his own autobiography, *Dreams from My Father*, Obama has Muslim sympathies (from his father's Kenyan side) and he cannot face the harsh truths that there are elements within the Islamic faith that encourage and promote violence and terrorism. Also Obama, based upon his Kenyan roots and heritage, has definite anti-western sympathies and holds views that oppose Western imperialism.

Obama is not actually supportive of terrorist actions killing and maiming Americans. But he understands that such actions may be as a result of America's military actions in Muslim countries like Iraq, Syria and Afghanistan. I believe that Obama was genuinely ashamed of previous American military actions in these Muslim countries, which explained why during his first term in office he was always going on these ridiculous and embarrassing "apology tours" to Saudi Arabia (where he allegedly bowed down to the ruling sheik) and other Middle Eastern countries apologizing for previous American military adventures.

Perhaps that is why Obama prematurely announced the withdrawal of American troops from Iraq and Afghanistan. In order to make amends to the Islamic world.

Perhaps Obama thought his love of Islamic fundamentalists and butchers would trump their hate for western values, western modernization, western liberalism, western democracy, western economic success, western dominance over the third world backward Islamic/Arab world, the western promotion of gender equality and sexual equality, western rule of law and western separation of mosque and state.

Perhaps Obama thought he could put garlands in his greying hair and dance around the maypole singing "Kumbaya, my Allah"and all America's troubles with radical Islamic terrorism would vanish.

Bottom line - the majority of Americans saw through Obama's not-so-clever ruses.

The majority of Americans saw the countless terrorist attacks in various European cities. They saw the beheadings, the torturing and killings of both Muslims and non Muslims by ISIS. They saw ISIS raping and enslaving women in Syria and Iraq. They saw Shiite Muslims battling and killing Sunni Muslims and vice versa in Iraq, Syria, Afghanistan, Libya, Yemen and in many other lands.

The majority of Americans could also connect the dots between ISIS in the Middle East and the various radical Islamic terrorist attacks committed on American soil.

If a terrorist has an Arab-sounding name. If a terrorist looks like a Muslim terrorist. If a terrorist claims loudly that he is serving ISIS, Allah and Islam. If a terrorist prior to an attack shouts "Allahu Akbar" (God is Great) which means "Allah is Greater than your God, your government, your religion and your people" with the intent of instilling fear in the hearts of non-believers. If a terrorist kills like an Islamic terrorist. If a terrorist leaves documents, Facebook postings or other social media indicia or videos, attesting to his radical Islamic moves. Then there is a very good chance that we are dealing with a radical Islamic terrorist.

And as a result, the majority of Americans concluded that within America there were real, clear and dangerous threats from radical Islamic terrorists and that Obama and his officials had dropped the ball, so they no longer felt safe with Obama and his politically correct apparatchiks, toadies and lackeys.

Foreign Policy

In response to widespread criticism of his mediocre foreign policy by Trump, the American military establishment and even by some members of the usually supine liberal press, Obama answered his critics by his characteristic meaningless platitudes delivered, of course, with oratorical flourish.

Basically, according to Obama, America still possesses the world's most powerful military force. We are still the world's sheriff. American is still respected internationally.

Obama implied with a sneer that he was still a very responsible Commander-in-Chief and Donald Trump was a know-nothing blowhard who was not fit to be President.

Typically, Obama did not apologize for his many serious foreign affairs blunders which critics rightfully argued had weakened the U.S. in the world, had helped produce some bad actors and consequences, and had allowed America's enemies to take advantage of Obama's blunders.

Here is a brief list of his major blunders:

Telegraphing in Advance America's Departure from Iraq and Afghanistan and Removing these Forces Prematurely

Whereas Obama had campaigned on withdrawing forces from Iraq and Afghanistan, the manner in which he had telegraphed his moves in advance to America's enemies - anti-American Sunnis in Iraq (the future ISIS) and the Taliban in Afghanistan - in both countries by providing firm dates of departure (Iraq by the end of 2011), instead of keeping the enemies off balance and guessing, was a major blunder.

In the case of Iraq, Obama was forewarned by his military advisers that the current Iraqi government was too weak to maintain any semblance of peace, and the same government had failed to bring the Sunni opposition into government. In the absence of significant American forces, conditions would be ripe for the emergence of a Sunni-led insurgent group, which became ISIS. Which in turn successfully invaded and occupied significant portions of Iraq and Syria. Thus further destabilizing both countries and leading to the horrible Syrian refugee crisis. These events were all reasonable consequences of Obama's non-action, indifference and incompetence.

In the case of Afghanistan, Obama, seeking re-election in 2012, promised to withdraw American forces in his second term. Unfortunately, that was a serious blunder as the current Afghan military was unable to defend itself against resurgent Taliban and al Qaeda forces. As a result of this blunder, Obama had to increase U.S. forces in Afghanistan in July of 2016, after having withdrawn them prematurely the previous year.

Libya: Obama's" Leading From Behind" Doctrine - A Doctrine of Weakness - So Obama

When you think of strong and dynamic American presidents you think of George Washington, Abraham Lincoln, Theodore Roosevelt, FDR, Dwight Eisenhower, John F. Kennedy and Richard Nixon and, though not a president, Colin Powell, head of the joint chiefs of staff, who developed the very effective military strategy in the first Iraqi Gulf War known as "shock and awe"- that is, massive and overwhelming strategic air power intended to destabilize and force capitulation early.

When you think of very weak leaders, the name of peanut farmer Democratic President Jimmy Carter comes to mind. He was the president who suffered from "lust in his heart" and believed America was suffering some kind of national malaise, a crisis of confidence.

More accurately the country was suffering from his weak and pitiful leadership. He was viewed by America's adversaries as so weak America was considered weak as well. Consequently, one of America's major enemies, Iran, was not deterred having its forces invade and occupy the U.S. Embassy in Tehran and seize fifty-two American diplomats and citizens as hostages for 444 days starting in November, 1979, during Carter's first and last term as president.

Similarly, America is suffering from a crisis of confidence in its leadership, namely Barack Obama - the weakest, most spineless and most pussy-whipped president in America's history.

With Obamacare, Obama was a reluctant and weak leader. Clinton, his Secretary of State, had to convince Obama to deploy American forces in Libya with their European and Arab allies attacking Libya, which ultimately led to the overthrow of Libya's leader Gaddafi.

One of Obama's officials then coined the Obama doctrine as "leading from behind," a very poor choice of words, but very appropriate for Obama's style of ineffectual and weak leadership.

Once again as in Obamacare, with Hillary playing the Pelosi role, someone else seemed to lead the American government as Obama cowered behind her pantsuit in the background.

But as with most Obama actions, neither Obama nor Hillary had a well thought-out plan in the event Gaddafi was overthrown. Consequently, Libya became destabilized as well.

Obama (together with Hillary) must take responsibility for the numerous tragic blunders relating to the Benghazi affair. The American embassy in Benghazi was not properly defended. The embassy was ill-prepared for a local attack. Additional armed forces or air cover were not called for. Four men, including U.S. Ambassador Christopher Stevens, were killed by Libyan al Qaeda terrorists. Obama (and Hillary) knowingly lied about the cause of the attack, citing an anti-Muslim video, which was patently false as al Qaeda forces had been planning this attack for days.

Syria and the Red Line

Perhaps one of Obama's worst international blunders was threatening Syrian President Bashar al-Assad, in August of 2012, with the intervention of American military forces in Syria if he crossed the "red line" of using chemical weapons against his own people while fighting opposition to his dictatorial rule of Syria. Assad ignored Obama's threat, called his bluff; Obama blinked, did nothing. America the superpower looked impotent and weak.

To add further insult Vladimir Putin, sensing Obama's and American weakness, became Assad's ally in supposedly fighting against ISIS, but in reality Putin deployed Russian armed forces against Assad's opponents in Syria, especially the Kurds, who were allies of the U.S.

Not only did Obama's blunders weaken American power and authority in the world, his negligence permitted Putin, running a second rate superpower like Russia, to become a major player in the Middle East on the side of Assad. Further, Obama's clear unwillingness to use military power to support American diplomacy has given Putin the confidence to slowly occupy eastern Ukraine and potentially other Eastern European countries which were formerly within the former Soviet Union.

U.S. - Iranian Nuclear Deal

This is another huge blunder. Democratic New York Senator Chuck Schumer has criticized this deal as a bad one for the U.S. and a very bad deal for America's ally, Israel. Schumer has suggested that Obama misled Congress and the American people in suggesting the U. S. has proper oversight over Iran, and that in the event of serious violations, the sanctions can be re-imposed. This is all BS.

Bottom line: Obama and Kerry were out-negotiated. Iran will receive over $150 billion dollars released to them and it will still develop a nuclear arsenal within ten years.

Obama's Other Foreign Affairs Blunder

In the twilight of his lame duck presidency, the arrogant and clueless Obama flew across the Atlantic to threaten Britons in advance of the Brexit or Remain referendum vote on the European Union.

Obama threatened that if Britain left the European Union, Britain would be forced to the end of the line regarding any trade negotiations with the United States.

The response by Boris Johnson, Tory Member of Parliament and head of the Brexit group, was swift and brutal. He dismissed Obama with a cutting and demeaning flourish.

Johnson referred to Obama as part-Kenyan, stating that the reason for Obama's infamous decision to remove the bust of legendary British Prime Minister Winston Churchill from the White House was because Obama viewed the bust as a symbol of the part-Kenyan President's ancestral dislike of the British empire.

Furthermore, Johnson objected to Obama injecting himself into a domestic political matter.

Britons on both sides of the debate applauded Johnson's cutting retort and dismissal of the thoroughly humiliated Obama.

The result of Obama's efforts? The Brexit forces triumphed. America was seen as a pitiful, impotent giant, an international laughingstock. Led by a second rate leader, possessing a second-rate mind. With no guts, glory or cojones.

Conclusion

Strip away the platitudes and oratorical flourishes of Obama's mediocre speech and, in reality, Obama's committed numerous serious blunders during his eight years as president.

Consequently, a majority of Americans believe that America is heading in the wrong direction with the economy, jobs, unfair trade deals, safety in the streets, illegal immigration, national security and the threat of radical Islamic terrorism, both at home and abroad. They are also concerned about America's perceived weakened role in a very dangerous and unstable world. Americans are also concerned as to whether America can still exercise its influence in the world in general and, more specifically, defeat ISIS once and for all.

July 28, 2016

Hillary Clinton's Acceptance Speech at the Democratic Convention - She Failed to Meet even the Lowest Bar Set by Her Harshest Critics

aka

The Worst Acceptance Speech Given by the Most Unpopular Democratic Presidential Nominee in Political History

* * * * * * * * * * * * *

I did not come by this very impartial and objective assessment lightly.

Before her speech, I knew that Hillary would not knock this sucker out of the park.

No way, Jose.

But I was open to Hillary perhaps hitting a solid single up the centre, between the centre fielder and the left fielder (in deference to the Sanders' people she must attract.)

Little did I suspect that she would whiff her speech so badly!

In assessing objectively both acceptance speeches, I turned for consistency to the coverage of both Conventions by the hard-working liberal folks at PBS, and especially their analysts and commentators: The Trump-hating conservative prig David Brooks of the *New York Times*, Mark Shields, an experienced old hand and amiable syndicated columnist, and Amy Walker, the calm, sharp and wise analyst who was a welcome complement to those two old farts.

Before Hillary's speech, the general consensus among these panelists was that these two conventions were like no others in the history of political conventions.

Usually, the candidate is not well known by most potential voters. And it is during these conventions that the general public learns, sometimes for the first time, about the candidate running for president.

In the case of Hillary Clinton, who has been in the public eye for the last 25 years, the public knows her all too well. Even those who have been living in a cave or under a rock for the last quarter century know about all her scandals, personal and political, to which she is a party:

Whitewater, allegations of sexual assault against Arkansas Bill, (see Juanita Broaddrick below), Travelgate, Hillary's disastrous D.O.A. health care plan in the '90s, "coming under sniper fire" in Bosnia", more sexual allegations against Washington Bill, Monica, the stained blue dress, impeachment, perjury, Hillary as Senator/ Secretary of State- alleged "pay for play" lucrative schemes between Clinton Foundation, Bill, its wealthy donors and Hillary allegedly using her government position to grease the wheels for such donors (see Clinton Cash below), the Saudi connection, the Goldman Sachs/Hillary unreleased papers, Benghazi, the anti-Islam video which allegedly caused the storming of the American embassy, Hillary's "negligent but strangely not grossly negligent" private emails of secret government documents, her 30,000 deleted emails, wiped expertly by the world's best email cleaners, Attorney General's Lynch secret meeting with husband Bill on the airport tarmac during an ongoing FBI investigation against Hillary, Obama prematurely interfering in the same ongoing FBI investigation and, more recently, Hillary rigging these very same Democratic primaries against Sanders and his millions of idealistic followers.

In 1978, while she was a nursing home operator in Arkansas, Juanita Broaddrick was allegedly raped by Bill Clinton while Clinton was Arkansas attorney general. Hillary allegedly tried to silence her a few weeks after the alleged sexual assault incident. Broaddrick went public with these allegations in 1999 and they have surfaced again in 2016.

In 2016 we are supposed to believe survivors of rape and, unlike Hillary Clinton, we are not supposed to silence them or intimidate them to silence. Hillary's treatment of this alleged rape victim may still come back to haunt her during this campaign.

Clinton Cash is a 2015 book by Peter Schweizer, investigating donations made by foreign entities to the Clinton Foundation, and how the Clintons have enriched themselves since leaving the White House by charging massive speaking fees.

This is one of many books and investigations by the *New York Times*, *Washington Post* and other newspapers which have detailed the unethical and potentially criminal use of Hillary's Senate and Secretary of State positions to enrich the Clinton family. These matters, also known as "pay for play" schemes, will continue to raise questions of Clinton's fitness for the presidency.

Everyone knows Hillary to a fault - actually as of last count 2,038 faults and climbing.

So the PBS analysts hoped that this one time, for the first time in 25 years, Hillary would show her real warm and fuzzy human side. Perhaps tell a self-depreciating joke. Perhaps talk about some of her difficulties. Perhaps show some remorse for rigging the Democratic primaries and "Berning up" the Sanders revolution.

Something.

Anything.

Personally I was hoping she had baked cookies for the thousands of Democrats in attendance.

The PBS analysts raised some very good points. Polls had shown that 70 per cent of the American people agreed that the country was heading in the wrong direction and they wanted substantive change, even from someone as unconventional and a little unhinged as The Donald.

These analysts also noted that Obama personally had good approval ratings at 50 per cent, but that Hillary's negatives were greater than Freddy Krueger, the facially challenged serial killer of Nightmare on Elm Street fame. Recall that Freddy used a glove armed with sabre-like razors to kill his victims in their dreams. Hillary used her iron gloved hand to kill the dreams of Sanders people live on TV.

To a person, the PBS people agreed Hillary would not benefit from Obama's personal popularity.

But in order to mobilize the Obama coalition (blacks, Hispanics, California Tesla liberals, left/lib guilty eastern urbanites) Hillary had to hew closely to Obama's policies (or lack thereof) for the last eight years (or appear to do so) while at the same time appearing to adopt some of Sanders' more radical cockamamie ideas to retain the support of his followers.

Hillary had to be both third term Obama and Sanders revolutionary.

In other words, Hillary had to lie her ass off to everyone.

Here I definitely agreed with Obama. No one running for president has ever been more qualified to lie and cheat than Hillary.

The analysts had other words of advice for Hillary and the TV viewers. They hoped that Hillary would reveal again for the first time what she truly and passionately believed in.

They also advised Hillary that the most powerful and effective speech is expressed in a soft-spoken, quiet, but firm manner, with a few well-chosen words.

Prior to Hillary's speech, her lovely daughter Chelsea had genuinely warmed up the crowd, singing the praises of her mom.

So then Hillary stepped up to the podium, to give the most important speech of her long, long, long, long, never, never, never, ending political career.

The Convention crowd was quiet, except of course, for the booing Bernie bros.

The TV audience collectively held its breath.

Hillary, as soon as she opened up her mouth, unlike in Jerry Maguire, she lost me at "Hello".

Instead of genuinely being touched by her daughter's very loving introductory comments, Hillary began to screech and yell. She was not humble or gracious. She was not soft-spoken and genuinely touched by Chelsea's warm intro. Instead, she initially came across as a loud, bull-headed Marine drill sergeant robotically summoning her troops to battle.

Hillary yelled with a fake fixed smile:

THANK YOU! THANK YOU FOR THAT AMAZING WELCOME!

AND CHELSEA, THANK YOU!

I'M SO PROUD TO BE YOUR MOTHER AND SO PROUD OF THE WOMAN YOU'VE BECOME!

THANKS FOR BRINGING MARC INTO OUR FAMILY AND CHARLOTTE AND AIDAN INTO THE WORLD!

Frankly, I could not believe how cold, distant, remote and robotic Hillary was. And this was when she was speaking about her daughter, son-in-law and grandchildren!

Being cold and dismissive of her philandering husband Bill - that I understood.

But to her own daughter and grandchildren?

After paying lip service to the speeches of Obama,

Michele Obama, Joe Biden (all speeches considerably superior to Hillary's own) Hillary turned to Sanders and with her typical straight face, she proceeded to lie and lie through her pearly white teeth, when she fake praised Sanders as follows:

"Bernie, your campaign inspired millions of Americans, particularly the young people who threw their hearts and souls into our primary. You've put economic and social justice issues front and center, where they belong. And to all of your supporters here and around the country, I want you to know: I've heard you. Your cause is our cause.

Our country needs your ideas, energy, and passion. That's the only way we can turn our progressive platform into real change for America. We wrote it together - now let's go out there and make it happen together."

Superficially these are very fine sentiments. The television camera panned to Bernie Sanders' box, expecting to see Bernie, smiling, clapping, doing a thumbs up salute.

Instead, there sat Bernie, stone faced. Angry. Compliant. Strangely subdued. Even pained.

As if Hillary's goons, prior to her speech, had threatened Sanders and his family to play ball and actively support the Godmother Hillary.

I had visions of Hillary's consigliere, husband Bill, playing the Tom Hagen/Robert Duvall role and gently threatening Sanders to come on board fully with Hillary or else.

One morning Bernie would wake up and the bloody head of his favorite pooch, Karl Marx, would be staring lifelessly at him from his pillow.

A few words about Bernie Sanders.

I like Bernie. I felt "the Bern." He started a revolution.

But then the evil Hillary got to him. She told him to take a dive. There was the destroyed Bernie up in the bleachers as Brando in On the Waterfront thinking to himself, "I coulda been a contender. I coulda been somebody, instead of a bum, which is what I am, let's face it......and what do I get? A one-way ticket to Palookaville!"

Bernie ran an incredible campaign, against tremendous odds, but as it was revealed he ran against a fixed primary system.

Here was this 75-year-old, independent white-haired Jewish junior senator from the obscure small state of Vermont, who developed a simple but powerful populist message that resonated with many young and old progressives throughout the country.

Bernie ran against the powerful "1 per cent" in American society, who to Bernie and his supporters caused income inequality and social injustice and tainted the political system and American life. He railed against Wall Street, the financial elites and unfair international trade deals for American working people, and he pushed for a higher guaranteed minimum wage of $15 per hour and free college and university tuition for children of the majority of Americans.

As a political independent, he ran honestly against the political elites of the right and the left. He garnered intense loyal support from predominantly young men and women and idealists and progressives of all ages in the Democratic Party. Bernie raised millions and millions of dollars from small donors as befit the anti-corporate thrust of his insurgent and populist campaign.

For months Bernie and his supporters complained that the so-called impartial DNC were fixing the primary elections against him. This bears repeating and repeating and repeating.

The WikiLeaks email disclosure proved conclusively that Hillary-controlled DNC officials engaged in dirty tricks to stop the Sanders revolution through voter suppression, press manipulation, badmouthing Sanders, the spread of disinformation, the undue influencing of super delegates by Clinton, years in advance, and many more such dirty tricks.

Going forward, this raises the most disturbing question: If Hillary Clinton and the Democrats would screw and fix the primary election of a fellow Democrat and millions of Democratic supporters (presumably with the full knowledge and implied consent of Obama and the Obama administration,) what dirty tricks would the Democrats, the Clinton forces and the Obama government do to prevent the free and democratic exercise of the rights of millions of American voters who chose to vote for the opposing Republican presidential candidate?

But back to Bernie Sanders.

This is what boggles my mind and I am sure infuriates Bernie's supporters.

For months Bernie complained about what he perceived to be the DNC's unfair and unjust practices and biased pro Hillary actions.

Once the WikiLeaks disclosure confirmed Bernie's worst fears of the DNC's official malfeasance, Bernie should have withdrawn his endorsement of the crooked Hillary.

Bernie said he was leading a revolution. He convinced millions of idealistic supporters that he meant what he said and what he had promised.

If Bernie meant what he said and was true to his word and the ideals of his revolution, Sanders should have publicly repudiated Hillary while giving his speech in front of millions of Americans at the convention.

Sanders should have called out Hillary for her lying and cheating and called upon his supporters to vote their conscience, and specifically vote for the Green Party, the Libertarian Party, or even the opposing party, to send a clear message that America no longer should support the lying and cheating Clintons.

Now that speech would have rocked the hall, shocked the country, and dealt some damaging blows to Hillary's campaign and perhaps would have re-energized the revolution to fight and win another time.

Sanders' failure to stand up for his ideals and the ideals of his revolution, led to his ignominious defeat and humiliation at the Convention. He bargained with the Devil.

As a result, his own people turned on him, ignored him and angrily booed Hillary throughout the Convention.

Sanders, rightfully so, left the Convention a broken, pitiful old man.

Many Sanders supporters refuse to vote or help Hillary. Their votes will go to the Green Party or they will stay home out of disgust for Hillary, or they will vote in retaliation for her arch enemy: The Donald.

The Democratic revolution is still alive. It just has moved on without Sanders.

The Content of the Hillary Speech

I watched Hillary's speech in its entirety. I have read her actual speech many times.

I listened to the pundits on PBS and I have read several critiques of her speech in several diverse newspapers and online journals.

I still believe my first impression and general impression were the most accurate.

It was a horrible, horrible, horrible, speech. The worst of both conventions.

The heavily-biased pro-Hillary liberal commentators on PBS - Brooks and Shields - agreed with me in part. They agreed that Hillary's speech was one of the two worst speeches of both conventions, the other being the Donald's speech. I will address that one in the next article.

Her presentation was abysmal. She screeched, yelled, hectored and lectured for over fifty minutes. It is no wonder she has such unfavorables with American men of all ages, colors, races, religions and ethnicities. Hillary came across as every man's worst nightmare; a typical screaming banshee of an ex-girlfriend, ex-wife or disapproving mother-in-law.

There is an old, but still worthwhile saying that "less is more." With Hillary, the converse is true.

The more Hillary, the less we can tolerate her.

Her speech would have been passable if she had stuck to a couple of defining issues and themes.

But as per Hillary, she showed terrible judgment and her delivery was even worse. As the liberal PBS commentators correctly complained, Hillary just provided a laundry list of every program and policy to every special interest group. Her speech was just a dispassionate checking off of the boxes: Hillary came across as being for everything, hence she really stood for nothing.

Drilling down to its basics, her message was "Vote for me, I have been in public life for over twenty-five years, I deserve to be president, while the other guy is a bombastic, self-centred, unstable demagogue."

Specifically, Hillary failed to sufficiently reach the 70 per cent of American voters who believe that America is heading in the wrong direction, many of whom have been swayed by Sanders' and Trump's clear populist and anti-establishment/anti-elitist messages.

Hillary cannot appeal to this large segment of the population because among the majority of average Americans and certainly among Sanders supporters, Hillary is Wall Street's girl.

As a New York senator she represented Wall Street, big banks, multinational corporations in Washington. Her senatorial campaigns and her primary and presidential campaigns have been largely financed by large financial institutions, investment banks, private equity groups, law firms, large corporations and high net worth individuals, many of whom are located in the New York/northeast/California and other major urban centres.

In contrast, Sanders' campaign was noteworthy for the large number of small individual donors.

Hillary Clinton has been handsomely paid by Wall Street banks for her speeches (the infamous Goldman Sachs talks come to mind and Hillary's non released comments.)

The large roster of Clinton Foundation donors comes from the same Wall Street financial pool.

It is no coincidence that Chelsea's first jobs have been with New York financial institutions. Her husband worked at financial powerhouse Goldman Sachs, then 3G Capital, and now he has set up his own hedge fund with the help of investments from Clinton Foundation donors.

Bill and Hillary paid for Chelsea's dream $3 million dollar wedding. They bought a multimillion dollar New York apartment for Chelsea.

So when Hillary tries to appeal to Sanders and Trump's supporters by talking about the evils of Wall Street, the horrible one per cent, and making the wealthy Wall Street banks and large American corporations pay through more taxes, it is once again pure lies, lies and more lies.

Simply, Hillary's speech was riddled with inconsistencies, half-truths and misrepresentations.

On one hand in order to curry favor with Obama supporters she spoke glowingly of how many jobs the Obama government had created. But then she tried to tack in the opposite direction and speak about the need to create jobs that had been lost in the recession and through bad trade deals (the opposing Sanders view.)

Recall Hillary was for Bill's NAFTA and Obama's TPP (Trans-Pacific Partnership) trade agreement, before she was against the TPP during the primaries because Sanders was opposed. And yet - during the convention Democratic Virginia Governor Terry McAuliffe, a close Clinton confidante, spilled the beans and said publicly that Hillary would support such a trade agreement.

Prior to her speech, Hillary had promised to close down coal mines and put mine owners and miners out of business. In her acceptance speech she inconsistently tried to reach out to these same workers - blue collar workers in mining and in oil and gas and related industries.

Then midway through her speech she flipped back again and started talking about the need to protect the environment and create clean energy jobs, which is a code word for closing down mines and restricting the production of oil and gas and gas-guzzling autos.

Hillary touched all the right issues: National security, fighting ISIS, crime in the streets and, the need for greater immigration (but not walls.) But again and again, Hillary failed to connect with the American people.

No one believed she felt their pain.

No one believed she even knew or cared that they were in pain. And frustrated and scared.

Hillary was simply not believable with any of these issues. She treated them all alike. Superficially, without passion or real concern.

She mouthed platitudes. She bestowed meaningless verbal goodies on different special interest groups.

Basically her speech was just so much sound and fury, signifying nothing of enduring substance.

The PBS commentators gave her speech a below average.

They were being kind and generous.

For all of her twenty-five years of public life and experience, it was a terrible, terrible speech given by a career politician with no judgment and no credibility.

I suspect that Hillary was counting on her compliant mainstream press, - aka the "Village of Idiots" - to spin her horrible speech and turn turgid prose and oratory into electoral gold.

And finally raise her in the estimation of the American voter.

My verdict: No amount of spin can raise Hillary in the eyes of a very angry and disaffected population who are rebelling against the status quo. Since Hillary is the status quo candidate, these rebellious hordes of Americans want to crush her on Election Day.

Let's rewind a bit…

July 22, 2016

GOP Convention - First 3 Days - Reality TV at its Finest!

✶ ✶ ✶ ✶ ✶ ✶ ✶ ✶ ✶ ✶ ✶ ✶ ✶

A close conservative friend of mine, after watching the first three days of the Republican Convention, said "This has been the worst Republican Convention that I can recall. Cruz should be shot for his disloyalty; the entire party needs to unify fast or this November will be a Hillary landslide."

As usual, I disagree. Yes, I agree Cruz was terribly disloyal. But shooting that little pinch-faced rodent is totally unnecessary. Also a tad redundant. Cruz committed political suicide on primetime TV, in front of millions of viewers.

Best episode of *"Survivor: Cleveland"* ever.

But we are getting ahead of ourselves.

My general impression of the first three days was that this was American politics at its messiest, rawest and most entertaining.

But also Republican politics at its most authentic, real and most democratic.

What Republicans did not want or need was a rerun of the 2012 Romney convention which was a boring, heavily scripted snooze fest, akin to a 4-day annual general meeting of the shareholders of an unexciting public utility corporation.

Trump, Republican billionaire outsider, is one of the most unconventional candidates in one of the most unconventional Republican or Democratic primaries in American political history.

Remember the first televised debate of the primaries in 2015, hosted by Megyn Kelly on Fox News and starring ten Republican candidates? It was like a weird version of *The* Bachelorette where the Bachelorette (Kelly) and one of her suitors (Trump) insulted each other mercilessly instead of flirting.

The ratings went through the roof. That show was watched by over 25 million Americans.

A "blood" feud between Kelly and Trump soon developed.

In effect, the whole debate/primary season led by Trump from day one became weirder, stranger and more compelling.

So it follows that the 2016 GOP convention, starring primary winner and presumptive GOP nominee Donald Trump and effectively produced by Donald J. Trump Family Productions, would be fraught with drama, uncertainty and bizarre and obnoxious behavior.

Such a GOP Trump convention would not follow convention. And it has not to a large extent. But then, in other ways, this Trump convention has followed some time-honored traditions, but with a characteristic Trump twist.

The Modern Family - Trump Style

Typically, the wife of the nominee introduces her spouse in an effort to humanize him. (Except when the nominee is Hillary and the spouse is a serial womanizer, so the better call is the dutiful daughter, Chelsea.) Since Donald Trump projected a tough, strong and sometimes crude and sexist image to the American public during the primaries, it was up to his family - including his current wife, Melania and his four children (Donald, Eric, Tiffany and Ivanka) from two different wives - to speak in favor of their husband or father.

Melania is a former model and stay-at home-mother. She is not an experienced public figure or public speaker. English is not her first language. Yet her speech was heartfelt, genuine and warmly received and she performed much better than expected.

The liberal anti-Trump media (the usual suspects of the *New York Times, Washington Post,* Clinton News Network, MSNBC and *Politico*), struck by the success of Melania, went absolutely ballistic and criticized her mercilessly for her speechwriter lifting about 7 per cent of her speech from a similar one given by Michele Obama in 2008.

Recall that Melania did not write this speech. She was reading someone else's words. It was not as if she had written a Pulitzer Prize novel that had plagiarized the best bits from another author.

Melania's speechwriter had lifted some positive messages and comments from Michele's speech, yet the crazy, biased pro-Hillary liberal press thought the greatest electoral fraud in the history of American politics had been committed on the electorate.

During the first three days, the three Trump children, Tiffany, Eric and especially Donald Jr. gave three very solid, assured and warm speeches. They spoke genuinely about the love they had for Trump, and how he was a fair but firm father who always wanted the best for them, and encouraged them to succeed in their chosen fields.

Donald Jr. was particularly strong in articulating Trump Sr.'s creative and entrepreneurial spirit, and his desire to lead America in creating jobs for those who have been forgotten by the elites or burned by bad free trade deals.

Donald Jr. believed that by creating good jobs, his father and his administration would be a unifying force in the country.

Contrast Eric and Donald Jr's articulate, warm and positive speeches about their father and his vision for the future with the mediocre performances by two experienced GOP leaders - Senator Majority Leader Mike McConnell and GOP House Leader Paul Ryan.

They both publicly endorsed Trump's leadership. Trump had after all won the majority of the delegates fair and square, after a brutally long debate and primary season. However, they both had difficulty reconciling their traditional Washington-based beliefs in global free trade, low taxes for the rich and reduced government entitlement programs with Trump's more aggressive anti-free trade approach and his populist appeal to the GOP base, on the basis of economic reforms versus red meat social conservative policies.

Their discomfort and ambivalence showed in their lackluster and mediocre speeches.

McConnell devoted most of his fire against Hillary. His only positive comments about Trump related to the fact that unlike Hillary, Trump as president would support the construction and development of the Keystone XL oil pipeline. Unlike Hillary, Trump would appoint conservative Supreme Court justices to the Supreme Court who would uphold the Constitution.

Admittedly, Paul Ryan had a difficult job. He had an obligation to support Trump, but at the same time he had an obligation to be mindful of the many vulnerable GOP senators and congressmen up for re-election in November, who may or may not be hurt by Trump's controversial candidacy.

Nonetheless, this opportunity called for a vigorous support for the party and for Trump on matters upon which Trump, the GOP base and the American people could agree. Instead, these two GOP leaders dropped the ball. They failed to appreciate, recognize and applaud the fact that Trump had tapped into serious populist economic anxiety in America among working class and middle income families and had won their support across all party lines

For months Trump had been campaigning against Washington political elites whom he argued were out of touch with average working American families. A large number of American people heard and responded favorably to Trump's message. Ironically, and notwithstanding all of Trump's success in the primaries, the Washington elites as represented by these two old-time politicians did not hear or appreciate this message.

On the other hand, other establishment GOP leaders and public figures, such as Newt Gingrich, Rudolph Giuliani and Chris Christie, were very solid.

Newt was very strong talking about the very real threat of radical Islamic terrorism that America faces both within its own borders from home-grown radicalized Islamic terrorists and outside its borders. He outlined in great detail the obvious threat of ISIS and its surrogates in the Middle East and in Europe and in many other parts of the world. The times call for strong leadership, not for weak leaders who fail to recognize these threats and even fail to define these threats accurately due to political correctness.

Giuliani, as a tough former New York mayor, talked about the need for safety and security in America, in its cities, in its communities and its schools. He argued that under Obama, America is less safe and the police who protect Americans have been mistreated and disrespected. Once again he contrasted effectively Trump's strong law and order stand and his support for the men and women in blue, with Obama and Hillary's weak stand on law and order in America and their tepid support of the men and women who keep Americans safe.

Chris Christie, auditioning for Attorney General, laid out a very strong case for indicting Hillary Clinton for allegedly violating the Espionage Act and for being grossly negligent in possessing sensitive national security documents outside the safe control and custody of the American government. In doing so, he called into question Hillary's fitness for being the president when she clearly put the national interests of the U.S. subordinate to her personal interests in keeping her private emails immune from federal Freedom of Information acts and public disclosure.

One of the most important speakers on the third night was Indiana governor Mike Pence, whom Trump had chosen prior to the Republican convention as his running mate. Admittedly, I had previously gone on record predicting that Trump would select the more experienced, more articulate and more charismatic Newt Gingrich.

I was wrong. Trump was right to choose Pence.

One of Trump's greatest strengths as a presidential candidate is also one of his major weaknesses - that is, he is not a Washington politician or political insider. In fact, Trump has never run for political office and he has no political or public service experience. Obviously his Washington outsider status has helped him blame genuinely and with authority the efforts of Obama and the political elites in Washington for screwing up the economy and making America less safe, and no longer great domestically, economically, militarily or internationally, any more.

In order to counter the justifiable criticism that Trump does not have any experience in running the government, Trump chose Pence, who has had both twelve years of legislative experience as a six term congressman in Washington and over three years of executive experience as the governor of Indiana.

Pence represents the more socially conservative wing of the party. By selecting him in advance of the convention, Trump tried to appeal to those conservative factions (the Cruz wing) who were not comfortable with his candidacy and his leadership of the party going into the general election. Trump also tried to minimize the inevitable discord he had produced with his scorched earth primary style of campaigning prior to the convention.

Mike Pence is a very personable, socially conservative guy with very strong family values. His speech was warm, amusing, self-deprecatory and, when necessary, very strongly critical of their opponent, Hillary Clinton.

Pence also genuinely supported several of Trump's key issues and slogans of making America great and safe again.

Or improving the economy and creating jobs as he had done successfully in his own state of Indiana.

Ironically, of all the speakers - including Trump's many family members - Pence went a long way to softening Trump's hard edges and making this tough law and order guy, also more palatable and friendly to the general public.

Trump always boasted that he was a dealmaker and that he would do great things in Washington.

The selection of Pence showed that Trump could compromise and bring on someone that he may not know well or share some of the same views, but for the sake of getting things done in Washington, Pence was the guy.

The Final Battle - Trump vs. Cruz

For me the highlight of the first three days was Trump brilliantly playing with Ted Cruz's head and manipulating Cruz into committing political suicide on national television, thus destroying his political career.

Also please note that Trump, the political strategist par excellence, has in effect modernized Sun Tzu's advice about how to deal with your enemies in *The Art of War.*

With Cruz, his key nemesis and primary opponent, "Keep your friends close, your enemies closer, and as for your most deadly enemy - give him a primetime speaking gig at the convention on national television."

Which is precisely what Trump did with Cruz, knowing in advance that Cruz would not specifically endorse or support Trump as president.

Remember that during the GOP primaries each candidate, including Trump and Cruz, pledged to support the winning nominee of the party.

One of Trump's greatest political strengths is his uncanny ability to accurately read a person, a crowd and a room.

Trump understood and correctly sensed that after a three-day full-on anti-Hillary hate-fest, the assembled GOP crowd at the convention, although not fully supportive of him, was almost unanimously united and fired up against the antichrist: Hillary Clinton.

Trump sensed also in that convention space that the angry Hillary-phobic crowd had come around to the idea that the only way of defeating her was to rally around Trump, who had won the nomination fair and square.

Trump knew that Cruz still harbored ill feelings towards him; Trump sensed that Cruz, deep down, was hoping Trump would fail against Hillary in 2016. Cruz was positioning himself to be the hardcore and principled GOP social conservative favorite in 2020, or even Trump's enemy in the GOP primaries, if Trump was the sitting GOP president at that time.

So Trump gave Cruz enough rope to hang himself, by giving him a prime speaking time on the third day of the convention.

As Trump predicted, notwithstanding that Cruz was given an honored time slot, his defeated opponent proceeded to ignore Trump and instead urged the GOP to vote their conscience, which was code for not voting for Trump.

When it was clear by the end of the speech that Cruz was not going to publicly endorse Trump, the crowd turned angry, booed Cruz off the floor and nearly threatened his wife. The GOP crowd both at the convention and at home were thoroughly disgusted with his betrayal, his lack of party loyalty and his lack of character.

Subsequently, Cruz's own Texas delegation turned on him and financial donors shut their doors in his face.

Trump had pulled off the impossible. He had vanquished his greatest foe and, in the process, had come across as a sympathetic character.

That was a brilliant gambit worthy of the great Sun Tzu.

And of course, great television.

July 29, 2016

Donald Trump's Acceptance Speech at GOP Convention = Good But Not Trump at his Best His Speeches At His Overflowing Public Rallies = More Appealing, Entertaining and Seinfeldian

★ ★ ★ ★ ★ ★ ★ ★ ★ ★ ★ ★ ★

As I head into the home stretch on a personal journey which has led me deep into the heart of American political darkness (I am referring to Hillary's black soul and cheating heart) I had hoped that Trump's acceptance speech at the Republican Convention on primetime television would, in itself, explain Trump's populist and popular appèal.

Unfortunately, it did not fully do that.

Unlike Hillary's deceptive and rose-colored view of the American economy and society, Trump painted a darker and more realistic picture. Reflecting the very real economic, financial, security and safety concerns of millions of American working class and middle income voters.

It was not a cheery "Good Morning, America."

It was also not an unrealistic, delusional Obamaesque "Hopey and Changey" vision.

Been there. Done that. Bought the Obama t-shirt and poster.

Both Sanders in his speech at the Democratic Convention and Trump in his acceptance speech correctly sensed that there was considerable anger, distress, frustration and insecurity in the land.

Trump's speech did what it had to do. It seriously outlined the ills of American society and the numerous failures of Obama/Hillary both domestically and internationally and Trump's responses to those problems.

The actual speech was well crafted.

David Brooks, the *New York Times* columnist and PBS network commentator - and frequent Trump critic - remarked that, having read an advance copy, he thought the speech as written was powerful.

Brooks of course did not like the way Trump delivered the speech that night.

Trump is not a great formal public speaker, especially reading from a prepared text off a teleprompter.

Trump's strength as a public speaker is his more conversational, natural and humorous speaking style. This is Trump at his best.

Later in this article, I will try to give you a better flavor of a more typical, popular and well-received Trump speech given at his many large rallies, based on the same themes and issues, but done in a more appealing manner.

Republican Convention Thursday Night

Ivanka's Introductory Speech

As with Chelsea Clinton's sweet introduction of her mother, Ivanka also warmly introduced her father and provided a little more insight into The Donald and his operations.

Ivanka made two solid points. She has worked for ten years with her father in a senior executive position, assisting him in acquiring land and/or buildings, and then building commercial buildings on such sites or renovating existing buildings.

Ivanka was very persuasive in reminding the American voters that, unlike Hillary, Trump has actually acquired, built and managed "stuff." Unlike Hillary, he did not make his fortune living off the public sector, as Hillary did, using her government position(s) or her access to power to earn outrageous fees for herself or large donations to Bill's

Clinton Foundation.

Ivanka also reminded the voters that Trump, over his entire career, has employed thousands of employees of all colors, religions and ethnicities, on the construction sites, in his buildings and in his companies. Throughout his business career, predominantly in multiracial and multicultural New York, Trump has never been accused of racism, prejudice or discrimination in his business or personal dealings. On the important stuff Trump has demonstrated that he is neither racist or prejudiced against any individual or group. On the contrary, Trump has actually provided good paying jobs to African-American and Hispanic employees throughout all his companies in the United States.

An important fact that the mainstream press conveniently likes to ignore.

Ivanka's other major point is that the majority of senior executives in the Trump companies are women. As a senior executive, Ivanka Trump has instituted a company-wide program of equal pay for equal work and a generous and supportive maternity leave policy.

These are other admirable Trump pro-female business practices and policies that the liberal biased mainstream press wishes to ignore when condemning Trump for being a sexist.

Trump's Major Acceptance Speech at the Republican Convention

I have read Trump's speech several times now. It is actually very clear, very well researched and obviously tough. According to Trump, these are tough and dangerous times.

I have been following Trump's speeches before the primaries, during the primaries and post primaries.

As with Sanders, Trump stayed with basically the same contrarian and anti-establishment messages he first developed out of the starting gate last June.

The Obama government and even the previous Bush and Clinton governments have ignored the plight of millions of hard working Americans who have lost their jobs to unfair free trade agreements which either destroyed their jobs or exported their jobs to foreign competitors.

Many of these Americans have never worked again or had to take part-time jobs. Those with full time jobs, the majority of them have not seen their salaries rise in years.

Trump railed against the fact that both the Washington-based Democratic political establishment and its opposite GOP number have forgotten and ignored these millions of Americans, and their struggling families and communities.

Trump argued both of these political elites have chosen globalism and liberal free trade internationalism at the expense of Americanism.

In other words, these political elites have put their interests, the interests of the lobbyists, the special interests they represent (Wall Street, Silicon Valley) and the multinational companies and foreign nations, ahead of the interests of working class and middle income Americans.

In this regard, Trump and Sanders are genuinely expressing the same populist message.

They are both fighting the status quo, the establishment and the poster girl for the status quo, Hillary Clinton.

To the liberal mainstream press Sanders is a revolutionary and a populist.

Conversely, the same yellow low-life liberal journalists misrepresent Trump to their readers and viewers as a fascistic, insane demagogue.

(**Trigger warning!!!** Political correctness check!!! Am I being racist for calling those low-life yellow liberal journalists yellow? Have I been caught red-handed? Then again has the crooked/corrupt Hillary blackened Obama's legacy? Is there a social justice judge in the house?)

Sanders' solutions were to boost minimum wage to $15 per hour and go hard on Wall Street and the 1 per cent and tax the shite out of them.

Hillary has no solutions because she does not see or really get the problem.

Trump will definitely not support the Trans-Pacific Partnership. (Hillary will cave.)

He proposes to renegotiate NAFTA and other agreements, enter into fairer bilateral trade agreements, attempt to bring back manufacturing jobs, discourage the exporting of jobs, promote the reduction of taxes on the middle class and small businesses, together with reducing government red tape (thus boosting creation of jobs), and proceed with the aggressive promotion of the production of oil, natural gas, mining and coal production. Full stop on job-killing climate change regulations and carbon taxes.

Note when Trump speaks genuinely about creating jobs, he is not just appealing to non college- educated white guys. He is appealing to men and women, young and old, white and black and Hispanic.

Don't the two latter groups want to have better paying jobs, fewer taxes and better opportunities to grow their businesses?

Trump's other better play is running hard against the crooked, corrupt and thoroughly disgusting Hillary.

In Trump's acceptance speech he criticized Hillary viciously for lying throughout her whole public life: Bosnia sniper fire, Benghazi anti-Islam video, deletion of her 30,000 emails on yoga, lying about not receiving classified government documents on her unsecured BlackBerries.

Also Trump played a winning card when he criticized Hillary for being so corrupt that during her four year term as Secretary of State, hundreds of millions of dollars flowed into the Clinton Foundation (and to Bill Clinton personally as speaking fees) from many donors (Arab nations, companies and high net worth persons,) many of whom were doing business with the U.S. State Department or U. S. Government, or who would benefit from having a friendly Secretary of State and potential president in their corner.

Trump also reminded everyone that Hillary rigged the Democratic primaries and gave the shaft to Sanders and his millions of loyal supporters.

Trump also hammered home that he believed Hillary was guilty of being grossly negligent in possessing classified government documents on her unsecure BlackBerries, yet she still walked? Recall Obama's Attorney General Lynch met with Husband Bill while the FBI investigation against Hillary was still ongoing. And Obama interfered with the same FBI investigation by proclaiming Hillary innocent before the investigation had been completed.

Trump scored big when he implied: Does the corrupt Obama believe the corrupt Clintons are above the law?

Another sleeper, and a winning issue for Trump

Tightening immigration from Mexico and dangerous Middle Eastern countries.

Hillary's open borders policy to the south, though a politically correct and feel-good liberal immigrant policy, has the effect of illegal immigrants taking jobs from black and Hispanic workers and legal immigrants. Trump may peel off some black and Hispanic voters on this score.

Also, Hillary's proposal to massively increase the immigration of unvetted Syrian refugees and possibly other immigrants from dangerous lands (i.e. the Middle East) feeds into the average American's legitimate fear of more deadly incidents of home-grown radical Islamic terrorism in America, which Hillary and Obama obviously fail to recognize and take seriously. Unlike the Trumpster.

In a rare moment I agreed with the anti-Trump pundits at PBS when they correctly suggested that Trump may have overplayed the crime in the streets/law-and-order issue at the convention.

I believe the economy and horrible Hillary are Trump's best and most effective cards to deal.

In order for Trump to cut into Hillary's traditional support, Trump has to stay on message and be disciplined with these major issues.

The problem for Trump going forward is to balance these clear and disciplined messages with his informal, at times improvisational, appealing, crowd-pleasing, entertaining and generally effective mass rallies, his social media tweets and the media's easy access to him.

Which breaks all the political rules and makes Trump a very formidable and unpredictable candidate. But an unstable one, as well.

I would like to close by discussing briefly the very successful, entertaining, and very effective Trump rally in Raleigh, North Carolina.

The Real Donald at Raleigh, North Carolina Rally

Trump's strength as a public speaker and as a popular and populist public figure is his more conversational, natural and humorous speaking style, where he makes the same point, repeats himself frequently, goes off topic, then loops back again, with wry and humorous asides and at times with feigned outrage and disbelief.

This is Trump at his best- most entertaining, most effective and most appealing:

"Well, look at that, I love you, North Carolina. I love you. I love you.

Unbelievable. You know. It's an incredible thing.

The system is totally rigged, but we are still happy to be together. The system is rigged.

What a system. What a group I tell you what....

And what is going on. Going on. Big league.

Big league. What we learned today. And last week.

From Bill Clinton going to the plane.

He just happened to be there.

Just happened to be there.

Essentially what was said. From what everyone thought.
She was guilty. She was guilty.

And it turned out that we are not going to press charges.
It is really amazing.

But I tell you. We have a rigged system, folks.

Hey, I tried to say that during the primaries. We were all together.

I won North Carolina. Big league.

Big league. Big league. Because of you...
We are stronger than ever.

We are fighting a very dishonest media.
We have a protester.

Get him out, please. We love our protesters.

Hey, you know, the only time they (the media) turn their cameras (to the large crowd to film the protester).

Look at the size of this place.

What do we want?

We want a good education.

We want a strong military.

We want strong borders.

We do want the wall.

We do want to keep our jobs in North Carolina.

We want to keep our jobs in North Carolina.
And I got a list of companies that have left North Carolina.

And they have gone to Mexico.

And it's a disgrace, what's happening.

It's a disgrace, what's happening.

We are going to stop it.

And it's not going to happen any longer.

We are losing our jobs.

We are losing our manufacturing.

We are going to stop the nonsense that is going on.

And it is so easy to stop.

We will stop it fast. Your heads will spin.

Remember that, your heads will spin...

We are going to knock the hell out of ISIS....

We have a president out campaigning for Crooked Hillary Clinton.

When he should be working on ISIS.

The threat is going to get worse and worse.

He should be working on trade.

He should be securing our borders.

People are flying in - coming from lots of places.

But from Syria.

No more.

No more.

We don't know who they are.

We don't know where they come from.

They have no documentation, no paperwork.
And who knows. And who knows.

We can't take any more chances, folks.

We can't take any more chances.....

Look at one person.

Down in Orlando.

One person. One person.

Look at what that one person has done to our country.

The gay community.

The LGBT community.

Was just - nobody can ever fathom what just took place.

That is just one bad apple.

We have many people coming in.

But there is just a small minority.

But there is something going on.

We have a leader that does not want to discuss the name of the problem.

The problem is very clear.

Radical Islamic Terrorism.

And it is a problem.

It is a problem.

(The crowd cheers, "Trump, Trump, Trump, Trump...")

....

We get Hillary Clinton who is weak, ineffective,
will never, ever be able to get the job done.
Her judgment is horrible.

Look at her judgment with the emails.
Who would do that?

Her judgment is horrible.

Oh right.

Her judgment is horrible.

Who said that about Hillary?

Bernie said her judgment is bad.

She's got bad judgment.

Okay.

Now let me tell you.

Whether it's ISIS?

Whether it's trade,

Whether it's borders,

Whether it's jobs,

It's going to be four more years
Of the same thing.
The last thing we need is another Clinton.

Or the last thing we need is another
Obama/Clinton in the White House.

We got a mess in this country.

We owe $19 trillion dollars in debt.

Soon to be $21 trillion.

The debt has doubled under Obama.

It's doubled.

We're sitting on a mess.

And it's got to be taken care of.

And it will be very quickly taken of.

And the best way is - jobs.

We got to bring back jobs to North Carolina.

We got to bring jobs back to our country.

It's got to be America first.

Not all these other countries.

That don't give a damn about us.

It's got to be America First.

America, America, America, America First

(The crowd chants "USA, USA, USA, USA!")

Obama is all talk and no action.

We need a president who is going to create jobs.

We need a president who is going to create jobs for African Americans.

We need a president who is going to create jobs for Hispanics.

We need a president who is going to create jobs for the whole country.

Remember that. Remember that.
Obama can't do that.

And Hillary Clinton will be worse."

This is the typical speech that Trump has given to large and very supportive and enthusiastic crowds through the primary season and during this final homestretch. There are good reasons why Trump is attracting large and enthusiastic crowds as his political momentum builds and expands towards the November election.

Here are some explanations:

For me, the effective art and exercise of politics starts with - and ends with - people.

Talking to them, responding to them, listening to them. Trying to help them out.

Unlike the "fake fixed smile and awkward in public" Hillary, Trump loves people. He loves to speak to people informally in large crowds. He is an entertainer and – hence - entertaining. He is at times funny, quick and charming. Other times he is outraged and dismissive of Hillary.

Clearly, Trump loves to make people laugh. As a public performer, he also likes to make people think and react strongly to his words.

Trump usually speaks from some prepared notes. He makes some basic points, but then in the midst of his speech, he goes off on tangents. He riffs on the basic themes of this campaign. Trump speaks naturally as if these ideas are just popping in his head. Sometimes they are.

Sometimes what he says is offensive. It gets him into trouble with the liberal media and his opponents.

But, on the other hand, he is always real and authentic. He means what he says and says what he means.

Trump says what people are thinking, but until Trump came along, these same people were afraid to state these politically incorrect thoughts in public.

For example, millions of people were thinking that despite all the happy talk coming from Obama, the Democrats and the GOP elites, things were not good on the ground. They were losing jobs or their salaries were stagnating. Their kids' futures were unclear.

But you would not sense that from Obama or from the Washington political elites as these political elites fought non-bread and butter cultural wars on Capitol Hill while the nation was reeling from an enduring economic recession in most regions of the country.

That is until Trump came along and questioned the advantages of these so-called free trade agreements to millions of average American working families.

Trump made it legitimate and acceptable to talk about the disadvantages of America's free trade agreements.

Trump also sensed that many Americans were concerned about their personal security and the loss of their jobs or suppression of their wages, due to the influx of over 11 million illegal immigrants from the south.

Trump said some offensive things about illegal Mexicans flowing through the unsecure southern American border.

He took flak for that.

But the existence of over 11 million illegal immigrants is a big deal to millions of Americans.

Trump made the topic of insecure borders and how to properly enforce such borders an acceptable topic for political discussion.

Contrary to the liberal mainstream spin and Hillary propaganda Trump is not a demagogue, along the lines of a Hitler or Mussolini, who just appeals to the worst instincts in people.

More accurately, Trump is one of the few politicians (the other exception being Bernie Sanders) who actually listens to the concerns and very real problems of millions of Americans and became their voice and their champion.

In the Raleigh speech above, Trump always talked about "we" must create jobs for North Carolina and for the country, not just "I."

What is also appealing about Trump is that he listens closely to his audience.

If a certain theme works - i.e. corrupt Hillary - Trump doubles down. Trump's observations and stories about Hillary's lies are dead-on. Hysterically funny. Even reaching Seinfeldian heights.

For example, Bill Clinton was caught with his "pants down" with Obama's hand-picked Attorney General Loretta Lynch.

We are talking here metaphorically, but then again it's Horn Dog Bill Clinton, so anything is possible.

Bill Clinton had a secret 39 minute private meeting in an airplane with AG Lynch while Hillary was under FBI investigation for possessing classified government documents on her private email system, allegedly in violation of the Espionage Act.

At the conclusion of the FBI investigation, FBI head Comey was to report to the very same AG Loretta Lynch.

The Hillary/Obama spin doctors were forced to put out the ridiculous story that nothing happened during their illicit 39 minute "meeting". They just talked about the grandchildren and golf.

In his Raleigh speech Trump went to town on this unbelievable fabrication.

Trump observed uproariously (I am paraphrasing here):

"Thirty-nine minutes to talk about grandkids and golf.

Look I have grandchildren. Eight of them. You ask how the children are? Fine. You show some photos. Here they are. Look how cute they are. That takes up about two minutes.

Then they talked about golf. Look I play a lot of golf. I know a lot about golf.

There is not much to say. How do you like that Adam Scott fellow?

Will Tiger make a comeback?

What did Bill talk about? His slice off the tee?

That golf talk took about two minutes. Then the rest of the time, what do you think they talked about? Hillary of course!

Unbelievable. Unbelievable."

By the end of this Trumpian riff, the crowd was hooting and laughing.

It was a brilliant, off the cuff riff. It showed Trump at his best, funniest and most appealing.

Trump has his obvious flaws. But unlike the flawed Hillary, Trump comes across as more genuine and authentic. Yes, Trump does say offensive things. But in a strange way, these off the cuff comments ultimately make Trump more appealing, popular and trusted than Hillary, who comes across as heavily scripted, humorless, mean, robotic, mendacious, tired, artificial - a thoroughly corrupted power-seeking political hack.

August 4, 2016

Hold on to Your Knickers, Campers, Because We're Going Out with a Trumpian Bang and not a Whimper

* * * * * * * * * * * * *

For me, this historical populist revolt against the Washington Democratic and GOP establishment elites did not suddenly arise with the "Make America Great" Trump Train or the "Feel the Bern" Sanders Revolution.

This revolt is greater than Trump. Greater than Sanders.

This populist revolt has been going on for many years.

For me, the seeds of understanding Trump's success in 2015 and 2016 were planted in a suburban Toronto, Ontario park on a very sunny day on July 5, 2013.

That day, I was a mild-mannered freelance columnist (emphasis on the free part) for a thriving international online media giant, the *Huffington Post.*

I had journeyed to this eastern suburb of Toronto to witness, report and comment on the phenomenon of Toronto's then-controversial Mayor Rob Ford and his followers, aka Ford Nation.

Ford Nation has been often described by liberal mainstream press as a bunch of angry, white non-college-educated working class folk who predominantly lived in the suburbs of Toronto.

That day I learned a few valuable lessons which I have applied to the unexpected rise of Trump. And his ultimate capture of the Trump White House. In no particular order:

1. The liberal elitist media are full of cow patties.

2. They have no idea what is really going on with the people.

3. Regarding Trump, in the case of the *Washington Post*'s E.J. Dionne, Eugene Robinson and George Will; the *New York Times*' David Brooks, Frank Bruni and Gail Collins, CNN's Don Lemon and *The Weekly Standard's* Bill Kristol: whatever they suggest, I go in the opposite direction for the truth.

4. The people, having been ignored and taken for granted for too long, have and are rebelling against the establishment leaders and are looking for champions for their own economic and financial interests.

5. The center-left and the center-right are not holding. Obama's all hopey-and-changey rhetoric - and no action - was no real solution. Hillary's platform is just more of the same: Obama, but worse. The GOP's trickle-down economy never trickles down to the people.

6. Trump's bread and butter issues have attracted appeal from average working class and middle income voters from both sides of the aisle.

7. Trump Nation, like Ford Nation, contains fiercely loyal citizens from all walks of life, and from all socioeconomic groups and from all races, colors, ethnicities and religions.

8. Trump is no more racist and sexist than Rob Ford and Trump Nation, like Ford Nation, will shock the clueless liberal pundits in November with its surprising strength among women and American non-white minority groups.

I know Americans like to believe that the United States is God's country. Echoing how both Puritan John Winthrop and President Reagan viewed the country as a "Shining City upon a Hill."

In other words, Americans believe that they are exceptional people. That they are the centre of the universe.

They are not.

I hate to break it to you, America. I studied at Harvard and lived and worked with the so-called "best and brightest," mostly dyed in the Kennedy wool, Democratic liberals.

You have a lot going for you, but you ain't so smart.

Best evidence: American liberals still support the corrupt, mendacious, power-hungry Hillary, without qualification.

Nor do Americans reside in the only "Shining City on the Hill."

But more importantly, Americans are part of an historic populist phenomenon.

From Ford Nation to Brexit and now Trump Nation.

The people want massive fundamental change.

They are mad as hell and they are not taking it any longer.

Contrary to the liberal urban elites in New York, Washington and L.A., the people are always right.

The people will win on November, 2016 and they will crush The Hillary and all that she represents.

However, when I shared this view on social media, the response I received was withering and dismissive.

"Hey, where's your empirical evidence", my critics bashed me. "The polls are all in Hillary's favor."

They continued, "You got nothing. Nate Silver, the polling genius, has given Hillary over 70 per cent odds to win."

My reply? "Nate Silver, are you frigging kidding me? He blew Trump big time and Big League, throughout the primaries. Silver did not understand Trump, or his support. And he failed miserably to predict Trump's success."

Whereas when Trump won the first New Hampshire primary in February, I called it for him to win the other primaries and crush either Sanders or Hillary in the fall. I also predicted the success of Brexit, weeks before the referendum vote.

I guess I must eschew taking the high road. The more philosophical approach.

I am still taking the road not taken. I am still sticking with my prediction on Trump.

But as a tough street kid from the mean streets of affluent Westmount, I guess it is time to get down and dirty and take this to the political alleyways.

Because Hillary and her people play fast, loose, mean and tough.

So to paraphrase Sean Connery in The Untouchables - and Obama, by the way:

"You wanna beat Hillary? Here's how you get her. She pulls a knife, you pull a gun. (Registered, of course. Second Amendment rocks!)"

"She sends one of yours to the hospital, you send one of hers to the morgue!"

She will try to rig the presidential election, like Kennedy's Daley did in Chicago for the 1960 presidential election.

(I am convinced that Hillary and her lackeys will use every dirty political trick in the books, as they did to beat Sanders by rigging the primaries. Come hell or Whitewater.)

So to beat her, Trumpsters, you have to be vigilant, expect the worst from her in terms of electoral dirty tricks, but in addition get all your supporters out to vote big time on election day and overwhelm her, as you did to Cruz in the GOP primaries.

That's the American Way!

Bottom line?

The election of 2016 reminds me very much of the election of 1980. Carter versus Reagan.

Carter, with a horrible, mediocre record to defend, focused on trying to character assassinate Reagan for being uninformed, inexperienced and unfit to be president. Does that sound familiar?

Also Hillary's support (like Carter's was) is indifferent and lackluster. She is a terrible and uninspiring speaker.

She is a horrible campaigner. Her crowds are meagre and listless. She is barely able to fill a one-bedroom apartment.

Her boring message is "whereas I may be a corrupt crook and a liar, with tons of scandals in my closet, Trump is worse because he is crazy and says offensive things about women and immigrants!"

It is no wonder Hillary has no popular momentum. And going to a Hillary rally is less fun than root canal.

I don't follow Hillary's Pravda-like propaganda machines, the dying *Washington Post*, *New York Times*, CNN, MSNBC or *The New Yorker* or the comparable propaganda polls.

I follow something quite revolutionary. It is called social media.

I have checked out hundreds of blogs and political sites for both Hillary and the Donald.

They are black and white.

The Trump people on social media are all fired up and pumped up. They love their man with a passion and they hate Hillary with equal passion.

I do not see or feel that same passion or emotional commitment to Hillary.

Accordingly, on Election Day, the Trump people will come out in force and contrary to the polls Trump will win in a landslide. As Reagan did in 1980, though all the polls had Reagan and Carter tied just prior to Election Day.

It will be 1980, déjà vu, all over again.

In that election, as in this election, the polls were wrong.

In this election Trump supporters have lied to the pollsters about their Trump preference.

How politically ironic! Lying Trump supporters will crush the lying Hillary.

That's karma, Hillary.

The people will always beat Hillary in the end.

As I write this note, about three months before the presidential election, the Trump/Hillary story is still evolving.

I expect there will be more craziness and weirdness on both sides.

I can hardly wait to plunge once again in this strange American pool of Darkness and Light.

Mitch Wolfe
AUTHOR

At Harvard, 1972.

Mitch Wolfe is a political analyst, writer and social commentator. Born on the mean streets of Westmount, Quebec, Mitch is a graduate of Phillips Exeter Academy and Harvard University.

Mitch's first exposure to American politics, up close and personal, was at Harvard where he roomed for four years with an Ayn Rand Libertarian (one of the founders of *Reason* magazine) and a Jewish Young Republican from Massachusetts. Mitch was actively involved in Harvard student government and the Harvard Institute of Politics. He wrote on student and community issues for the Harvard Independent with his friend, fellow student leader and current nominee for the Supreme Court of the United States, Merrick Garland.

Subsequent to Harvard, bitten by the political bug, Mitch spent many years organizing and managing political campaigns in Canada and following and commenting on American political campaigns and politics. He also successfully financed numerous Canadian and American television series, films and documentaries. He also spent some crazy times in Hollywood, on the board of directors of Lionsgate Entertainment.

Mitch Wolfe's true passion is covering and commenting on politics and culture with humor and bite. He prides himself on being a populist, a contrarian, fiercely independent and oftentimes politically incorrect. And though he is currently describing himself in the third person, he never takes himself too seriously.

Mitch first starting writing conservative articles on American, Canadian and international politics for the left wing *Huffington Post* several years ago. His writing gigs have led to public speaking engagements and frequent political commentary on American radio and Canadian television.

He would like to humbly stand in the shoes of such iconic political writers as Norman Mailer (*The Armies of the Night*) and Hunter S. Thompson (*Fear and Loathing on the Campaign Trail '72.*)

Though there has been considerable fear and loathing in this very bitter, divisive and polarizing campaign season, Mitch always tries to inject his singular humor, humanity and occasionally biting wit to the serious matters at issue.

Mitch Wolfe has written for the following online journals, sites and blogs: *Huffington Post, iPolitics, The Rebel Media, Canada Free Press, CIJNews, the Women's Post* and the *YummyMummyClub*

For my wonderful dad, Aubie, who gave me his big heart and love of life and laughter.

And for my mom, Annalee, one very tough, feared and respected character; she gave me the self-confidence to be resilient, fearless and single-minded.

Acknowledgments

One evening the well-known Aussie-born publisher Marnie Kay turned to me and shocked me by telling me that she was very political. She loved my writing. I made her laugh. I provoked her. She loved my voice and she could not get my voice out of her head. And she wanted to publish me.

Thank you, Marnie, for your vision, smarts, creativity, enthusiasm and drive. It has been an incredible ride.

I want to also thank my editor and good friend, Rick McGinnis, a very talented writer, commentator and photographer in his own right. He provided very astute guidance and insight throughout this very enjoyable process. At times his editing was light. Other times, firm. Always, bang on. It has been an honor.

My friend Gary Bellinger spent hours and hours reading my pieces online and he played an invaluable role as a sounding board and another pair of eyes on the material.

I also want to thank my dear friend Anne LeBarr. Though she is a multi-generational dyed-in-the-wool, "pure laine" liberal, she somehow found the patience to put up with my frequent conservative rants and raves. She found the humor, humanity and passion in my writing and kept me open to opposing views. She encouraged me to write this book. I will always be grateful.

I also want to acknowledge my good friend, the departed but never forgotten Rob Ford. Through his eyes I understood his populism and his unique and rock-solid popularity with all races, colors, religions, ethnic groups and income groups.

When Donald Trump called on the Washington elites to "Stop the Gravy Train," one of Ford's signature slogans, I knew I was on the right track with this book.

And when Brexit rebelled against the arrogant, unelected, out of touch E.U. elites, I knew that Ford Nation had gone global.

62404228R00212

Made in the USA
Charleston, SC
14 October 2016